Lord Byron
Romantic Poet & Warring Lord
A man with two distinct dissociative identities

An informative walk in the footsteps of Lord George Gordon Byron from an uneasy childhood and adolescence to the blooming of a poetic genius, freedom fighter, revolutionary statesman and martyr to The Cause of Greek Liberty

Stephanie Freeman BA (Hons) MRS

© 2024

PREFACE

It was at Woking Grammar School that I first discovered my passion for History and English Literature. I graduated from Exeter University with a degree in Economic History and The American Revolutionary War as my specialist subject.

Not surprisingly, with Lord Byron's ancestral home on my doorstep, I have been a frequent visitor to Newstead Abbey over the past fifty years! In 2022, I signed up as an in-house volunteer. Perhaps not surprisingly, following a career in market research and with a naturally investigative mind set, I sought to discover the truth about George Gordon Byron's life - both at home and abroad. This soon developed into a passionate desire to walk in the footsteps put down by MiLord from his birth in 1788 to his death in 1824. To determine the true facts about his life and record my findings in a concise easy going style. I have made the content as accurate and truthful as I can. I hope to have avoided the myths which surround his lifestyle, but recognise that this is not always easy, or indeed possible! His memoirs were burnt to ashes. However, we still have not only his prolific correspondence, his journals, conversations and observations to reflect upon, but also the memoirs and literary works of his contemporaries.

This is not an academic tome but a distilled thematic and historical approach which picks up on a number of different subjects which illuminate his life and legacy.

In celebration of Byron's bicentennial, the book is launched at a special low price of £9.99 and profits will subsequently be donated to the Byron charities in his ancestral homeland.
Welcome to Byroniana. I hope you enjoy reading this book as much as I enjoyed writing it!

CONTENTS

1. LORD GEORGE GORDON NOEL BYRON TIMELINE

1788: On January 22nd, George Gordon Byron was born to Catherine of Gight and Captain John Byron in a lodging house at 16 Holles Street London. He was born with a deformed right foot which was widely referred to as a club foot.

1789: Captain John Byron deserted Catherine and she took baby George to lodgings in Aberdeen, Scotland. He was a pupil at Aberdeen Grammar School. He left Scotland in 1798, at the age of ten.

1791: Captain John 'Mad Jack' Byron died in France of tuberculosis.

1798: George Byron became the 6th Lord Byron when he inherited Newstead Abbey in Nottinghamshire on the death of his great-uncle William - 5th Lord Byron. At the age of ten, Byron first visited Newstead Abbey, his ancestral home.

> *"Through thy battlements Newstead, the hollow winds whistle;*
> *Thou, the hall of my fathers, art gone to decay."*
> *(George Byron : On leaving Newstead 1803)*

1799: The Byrons moved to London and young George attended Dr Glennie's school in Dulwich.

1800: Byron spent the summer holiday in Nottingham and at Newstead Abbey.

1801: Lacking the necessary funds, Byron's mother was forced to apply to King George III for a grant to pay for her son's education. Byron was educated at Harrow School (1801-1805).

"His heart is good and his talents are great. I have no doubt of him being a great man" (Catherine Byron)

1803: With no money available to restore the semi-derelict ancestral home, Catherine Byron rented Burgage Manor in Southwell, Nottinghamshire. Newstead was leased to Lord Grey de Ruthyn.

During the summer holidays, Byron stayed with Owen Mealey, the Newstead steward. He met his first love, Mary Chaworth of Annesley Hall, and refused to return to Harrow in the Autumn term. She firmly rejected him however, in favour of John Musters, and famously said to her maid –

"What! Do you think I could care anything for that lame boy."
1804: Byron spent more time at Burgage Manor and established a lasting friendship with Elizabeth and John Pigot.

1805: Byron attended Trinity College Cambridge (1805-1808). He outsmarted the college authorities when he took Bruin the Bear with him, in defiance of the rules that banned students from keeping dogs in college.

Byron established strong friendships with fellow students and experienced a *'pure, love and passion'* for John Edleston, a choirboy at Trinity.

1806: Byron spent much of his holidays in Southwell where he organised theatricals and published his first poetry. *Fugitive Pieces* was privately printed and then quickly withdrawn.

1807: *Poems on Various Occasions* was privately printed and *Hours of Idleness* was published. The latter was ridiculed in the Edinburgh Review the following year. Byron retaliated with *English Bards and Scotch Reviewers* (published in 1809).

Byron left University and resided on and off at Newstead Abbey between 1808 and 1814.

1808: Byron was a huge animal lover. This love was epitomised in "Epitaph to a Dog"written upon the death of Boatswain (Bo'sun) his favourite Newfoundland dog who died of rabies at the age of five. Boatswain was buried under an elaborate monument. Byron's wills specified that he wished to be buried alongside Boatswain in the large tomb underneath - without ceremony.

1809: Byron took his seat in the House of Lords - as a (Radical) Whig.

On July 2nd he embarked upon a Grand Tour of the Mediterranean along with his university friend, John Cam Hobhouse, and Newstead servants Joe Murray, William Fletcher and Robert Rushton.

Due to the impact of the Napoleonic Wars, they visited Portugal, Spain, Gibraltar, Sardinia, Malta, Albania, Greece and Turkey.

1809: In Malta, Byron was persuaded by British Naval and Diplomatic Intelligence to visit Ali Pasha at his palace in Tepelene (in Albania). It was here that he commenced writing *Childe Harold's Pilgrimage*. The party then moved on to Greece and Constantinople (Istanbul).

1810: Byron swam around three miles (approaching five kilometres) across the Hellespont (Dardanelles) in a mere one hour and ten minutes.

He stayed at The Capuchin monastery in Athens, where he met Nicolo Giraud. He employed him as his translator and head servant while he continued his travels abroad.

1811: Byron wrote *Hints from Horace* and *The Curse of Minerva* whilst in Athens. The latter denounced Lord Elgin's actions in removing the marbles (ancient Greek sculptures) from the Parthenon and Acropolis in Athens.

Byron returned to England on July 14th. His mother died on August 1st followed by two of his closest friends - Charles Skinner Mathews (drowned in the river at Cambridge) and John Edleston (died of consumption).

He resided initially at Newstead Abbey and, after three months, returned to London to live at 8, St James's Street.

1812: On February 27th, Byron made his maiden speech in the House of Lords in response to The Frame Breakers Bill. This applied the death penalty to Luddites convicted of destroying the new machinery that caused unemployment and starvation amongst Nottingham Lace weavers.

Childe Harold's Pilgrimage cantos 1 and 2 were published by John Murray Publishers in Mayfair, London. It sold out in three days, which prompted Byron to exclaim -

"I awoke one morning and found myself famous."

Its outstanding success meant that Byron was besieged by women, including Lady Caroline Lamb. At the start of their tempestuous affair, she famously exclaimed that Lord Byron was *"Mad, Bad and Dangerous to know."* Having rejected Caroline, he embarked upon an affair with her friend Jane Harley, Countess of Oxford.

He proposed marriage to Anne Isabella (Annabella) Milbanke - but was rejected.

1813: Byron made his last speech in the House of Lords.

The friendship with his half-sister Augusta Mary Leigh had become much closer and more controversial.

1814: Byron and Augusta spent time together at Newstead and Six-Mile-Bottom in Cambridgeshire - the family home of George and Augusta Leigh.

The Corsair proved a resounding success - 10,000 copies were sold on the first day of publication. Later in the year, Byron proposed marriage again to Annabella Milbanke - and his offer was accepted. He travelled to Seaham in County Durham, where they were to be married.

1815: The marriage took place on January 2nd and they lived together at 13, Piccadilly Terrace, London. Byron worked at Drury Lane Theatre and Augusta Ada was born on December 10th.

1816: The marriage failed. On January 15th, Annabella left the London house and took their daughter with her. The couple never met again. Byron wrote two poems about the separation - *"Fare Thee Well"* and *"A Sketch from Private Life."* Annabella forbade any form of contact between Byron and his daughter.

"Oh, my poor dear child, my dear Ada! My god, but I could have seen her!" (Byron)

The 28 year old Byron left England on April 25th, never to return. He felt isolated, ostracised and alienated by the hardening of public attitudes toward his lifestyle, sexuality, relationship with his half-sister, a broken marriage and crushing debts.

Byron travelled to Geneva where he met up with Percy Bysshe Shelley, Mary Godwin and Mary's stepsister, Claire Clairmont. At Villa Diodati on Lake Geneva they held a competition to see who would write the best horror story. It was here that Frankenstein's Creature was born and Vampires re-vamped. Claire Clairmont had met Byron before his self-exile and returned to England pregnant with his child.

1817: On January 12th, Clara Allegra Byron was born. Byron had moved to Italy and lived for three years in Venice. In December, he was informed that Newstead Abbey had been sold – and thus his years of financial insecurity were at an end.

1818: In Venice, Byron's writings were often influenced by his surroundings and it was he that gave the English name to the Ponte dei Sospiri -

"I stood in Venice on the bridge of Sighs, a palace and a prison on each hand." (Byron)

Byron frequently bragged about sleeping with countless women during his time in Italy.

1819: Byron met and fell in love with the recently married Teresa Guiccioli - it was to be his last love. He took on the role of Cavalier Servente (gentleman in waiting and lover) and accompanied her to her family home in Ravenna.

1820: In February, Byron moved into the Palazzo Guiccioli. In July, Teresa was granted a separation from her husband by papal decree. She was obliged to move back in with her father - Count Ruggiero Gamba. Byron became acquainted with her brother, Pietro Gamba, and joined The Carbonari - a secret revolutionary society. However, the planned insurrection failed and ended all hopes for the liberation of Italy from the Austrian Empire.

1821: Teresa's father and brother were arrested and sent into exile. Byron moved to the Casa Lanfranchi in Pisa where he met up once again with the Shelleys and their circle of friends. It was here that Byron first met Edward Trelawny. A novelist and adventurer, he joined Byron in the fight for Greek independence.

1822: Lady Judith Noel Milbanke died and Byron incorporated the Noel coat of arms into his own armorial bearings. From then on, he signed his correspondence 'Noel Byron'.

In April, Byron heard the news that his daughter Allegra, only five years old, had died in the convent at Bagnacavallo, Ravenna.

On July 8th Percy Bysshe Shelley and Edward Williams drowned in a boating accident in the Bay of Spezia.

Byron moved to Casa Saluzzo in Genoa where *The Vision of Judgment* was published in the radical journal 'The Liberal'.

1823: With increased political awareness, Byron ultimately turned his back on poetry, to invest his reputation and money in The Greek War of Independence. Byron joined the London Greek Committee and sailed to the Greek island of Cephalonia, to await further instructions.

1824: On January 5th Byron finally arrived in Missolonghi and with a strong commitment to 'The Cause', he experienced his final transformation into a New Age Statesman and Political Leader. Byron spent a significant amount of his personal fortune in order to provide arms and medical supplies and repair ships in the Greek fleet. He set up his own military squad of Souliotes (Albanians) and an artillery brigade of foreign volunteers.

Lord Byron died in Missolonghi a 'martyred hero' on April 19th 1824 at the age of thirty-six. He died of what is now speculated to have been a malaria relapse and exsanguination (a severe loss of blood).

"This misfortune that has befallen us is terrible and irreparable. Lord Byron is dead, your friend, and my friend and father, the saviour of Greece is dead. I cannot tell you the inconsolable grief of his friends and of the whole of Greece. In the flower of his prime." (Pietro Gamba)

His death secured sympathy and support by western nations for the war effort. Byron is remembered as generous and brave; a man who gave all he had, including his life, to Greece – an indisputable hero. *"I have given my time, my means, my health – and now I give her my life – what could I do more."* (Byron)

News of Byron's death was published on the front page of The Times. However, many religious and cultural institutions refused to honour him upon the return of his body to England, due to his 'questionable morality.'

"The Dean of Westminster refused burial in the Abbey. For many years the open profligacy of his life prevented his commemoration in the Abbey." (westminster-abbey.org)

Lord Byron was buried in the family vault in St Mary Magdalene church at Hucknall Torkard, Nottinghamshire. It was not until 1969 that a memorial stone provided by the Poetry Society was placed in the South Transept; Poets' Corner. It adjoins the memorials to Dylan Thomas, Lewis Carroll and D.H. Lawrence.

Since 1845 the statue by Bertel Thorvaldsen, commissioned by John Cam Hobhouse and John Murray for Poets' Corner in Westminster Abbey, has stood proudly in the Wren Library at Lord Byron's alma mater, Trinity College Cambridge.

It depicts Lord Byron sitting amongst the debris of a Greek temple with a copy of *Childe Harold's Pilgrimage* in one hand and a pencil in the other. The imagery is one of calm contemplation.

Fig1
Statue of George Gordon, Lord Byron by Bertel Thorvaldsen (1830-34)

Thus In 2024, the bicentennial of the death of Lord George Byron, this statue conjures up not only 'The Genius of Poetry' but also 'The Heroic Statesman' and 'Martyr to the Greek Cause of Liberty'.

2. ANCESTRY

The Burun family arrived in England with William the Conqueror in the 11th century. Their paternal ancestors were from Normandy and Ralph 'de Burun' is listed as a landowner in the Domesday Book (1086). By the end of the 12th century they had acquired Clayton Hall near Manchester. Colwick Hall in Nottinghamshire was acquired in the 14th century and the Manor of Rochdale near Manchester was purchased in 1638.

1st. Sir John Byron of Colwick (died c. 1567)
The first Sir John Byron was an English nobleman and politician of the Tudor era. He lived at Colwick in Nottinghamshire. In 1540, Henry Vlll granted him the dissolved monastery of Newstead Abbey (for £810) in recognition of his loyalty. Sir John dismantled the church using the stone to convert the Priory into a Country House - owned by the Byron family for the next 280 years.
Sir John was Constable of Nottingham Castle, Lieutenant of Sherwood Forest, Sheriff of Nottinghamshire and Derbyshire - and Member of Parliament for Nottinghamshire. In 1543 Sir John was made steward of the royal Manor of Rochdale.
Sir John Byron married Isabel Lemington (no issue) and Elizabeth Casterden (one daughter and three sons).

2nd. Sir John Byron of Clayton and Newstead (died c. 1600)
An Elizabethan nobleman and politician, he was known as Little Sir John with the Great Beard. He lived initially at Clayton Hall, Manchester and moved to Newstead Abbey in 1567. He was knighted by Queen Elizabeth in 1579. Married to Alice Strelley, he fathered 3 boys and 6 girls. His eldest son died before him in 1587 and he was succeeded by John.

3rd. Sir John Byron (died c. 1623)

Debts mounted and the Manor of Colwick was sold along with estates in Lancashire. Sir John welcomed King James I to Newstead Abbey. It provided good hunting grounds and a base to explore the haunts of Robin Hood. He took little part in public affairs, spending time looking after his wife who suffered from mental health issues. John Byron married Margaret Fitzwilliam and fathered five sons and five daughters.

4th. Sir John Byron of Newstead (died c. 1625)

A Knight of Bath, he married Anne Molyneux. They are estimated to have had 17 children (12 boys and 5 girls).

5th. Sir John and 1st. Baron Byron of Rochdale (died c. 1652)

One of Charles I's foremost Royalist commanders (Cavalier General) during the Civil War. The Manor of Rochdale was purchased in 1638. Sir John was elevated to the peerage as Baron Byron of Rochdale five years later in 1643. He had studied at Cambridge and taken The Grand Tour around Europe.

He was a knight of Bath and held various positions as an MP, High Sheriff for Nottingham and Lieutenant of the Tower of London. It has been said that Sir John helped Charles I to lose the Battle of Marston Moor by charging without orders. Newstead Abbey was confiscated and Sir John Byron was exiled.

Married to Celia West and Eleanor Needham, he died without an heir, in Paris in 1652.

Richard 2nd. Baron Byron of Rochdale (died 1679)

Brother of John 1st Baron Byron, Richard was also a Royalist and supporter of Charles I. He inherited Newstead Abbey in 1652 along with the office of Governor of Newark. Facing huge legal and financial problems – he sold the Royston estate in Lancashire and stripped the Abbey of much of its contents.

He was married to Elizabeth Russell (six children) and Elizabeth Booth (no children).

William 3rd. Baron Byron of Rochdale (died 1695)
Married to Elizabeth Chaworth, daughter of John Chaworth, 2nd Viscount Chaworth. They had five sons - but sadly four died in infancy. They lived at Bulwell Wood Hall (originally the house of Richard 2nd Baron Byron) and inherited Newstead Abbey in 1679. They left it in a much healthier financial position.

William 4th. Baron Byron of Rochdale (died 1736)
Born at Newstead Abbey. He was a collector of paintings, a talented amateur painter and gifted musician.
Three advantageous marriages took place - firstly in 1703 to Lady Mary Egerton; 1706 Lady Frances Wilhelmina Bentick - and finally in 1720 the Honourable Frances Berkeley - the mother of his children (five sons and one daughter).

William 5th. Baron Byron of Rochdale - The Gothick Lord (died 1798)
William inherited Newstead Abbey in 1736 at the age of fourteen, whilst at Westminster School. He was removed from school at sixteen, and sent into the Navy. Coming of age in 1743, he left the Navy. He was elected Grand Master of the Premier Grand Lodge of Freemasons of England.
Throughout his life, expenditure outstripped income. Money was spent on extending his father's art collection and building Gothic follies - the Folly Castle (with 4 guns), the Battery (with 7 guns) and the Kennels Castle.
In January 1765, he (accidentally) killed his cousin and neighbour William Chaworth in a duel with swords at the Star and Garter tavern in Pall Mall. He was tried and judged guilty only of manslaughter - and released.

He continued to visit London frequently and brought back parties of friends to shoot ducks or enjoy mock naval battles from the Battery on the shore of the Upper Lake. The 20 gun schooner and five other boats were manned by professional crews and servants.

Despite finances in a dire condition, he attempted to maintain the estate and treated tenants and servants well. In the 1770s, he was forced to sell a large number of the 4th Lord's art collection (including Rubens, Titian and Canaletto); the Brass Eagle Lectern and candlesticks (now in Southwell Minster). This was followed by a 6 Day sale at Newstead Abbey. He sold the colliery rights in Rochdale and then became an 'eccentric and misanthropic' recluse. He allowed the Abbey to fall into disrepair.

He married Elizabeth Shaw in 1747 with whom he had four children (two boys and two girls). His sons died prematurely - and he outlived his grandson who was killed by cannon fire at the siege of Calvi in Corsica. His wife left him after the 'Great Sale' and took with her their only surviving child, Caroline. William Byron died at the age of 75. As a result of the stories told following the duel, and his financial difficulties, he was referred to as the 'Wicked Lord' and 'The Devil Byron' after his death.

3. FAMILY VALUES

Vice-Admiral John Byron (1723-1786)

A British Naval officer and explorer, John Byron fought in battles in the American War of Independence and circumnavigated the world.

He was given the nickname Foul-Weather Jack because he often encountered adverse weather conditions at sea.

Fig 2
Admiral 'Foul-Weather Jack' Byron by Joshua Reynolds c.1748

It was claimed that sailors would rather jump ship than sail with Foul Weather Jack. He was appointed governor of Newfoundland. Byron Bay (New South Wales, Australia) was named in his honour by Captain James Cook in 1770.

The second son of Frances and William Byron, 4th. Baron Byron, he married Sophia Trevannion in 1748 and had nine children (of whom three died in infancy). Their eldest son was John Byron and George Anson Byron was his younger brother.

Captain John Byron (1757-1791)

John Byron was the sixth child and eldest son of the Vice-Admiral John Byron. He was a British Army officer and Captain of the Coldstream Guards. He was known to be a deplorable gambler, a notorious womaniser, and a spendthrift with mounting debts. John Byron married Amelia Osborne, Marchioness of Carmarthen. They had three children, two of whom died in infancy. His wife died in 1784, leaving him a widower with a one year old baby daughter and a mountain of debts.

In search of an heiress, he married Catherine Gordon, heiress of Gight in Aberdeenshire. He spent her fortune paying off his debts. They had one child - George Gordon, born on January 22nd 1788. Acrimonious quarrels resulted in baby George seeing his father for the last time aged two years. Jack left for the continent in 1790 to escape creditors and debtor's prison. He died in his sister Fanny's house (Frances Leigh) in Valenciennes, France in 1791. Had he survived he would have been next in line to inherit his uncle's title. Instead it fell to his ten year old son George Gordon in 1798.
"I was not so young when my father died – but that I perfectly remember them and had very early a horror of matrimony from the sight of domestic broils." (George Gordon Byron)

Catherine Gordon of Gight (1764-1811)
Daughter of George Gordon, Catherine Gordon was the 13th Laird of Gight Castle, situated in the Formartine area of Aberdeenshire. She was descended from the Earl of Huntley and Lady Jane Stuart, daughter of King James I.

Catherine married John Byron in 1785. He had massive debts and had been disinherited by his father. A fortune hunter, he was delighted to meet Catherine while on holiday in Bath. He quickly ran through most of the £23,000 she had brought to the marriage and sold Gight Castle to pay his debts.

After the birth of their son George Gordon, Catherine took the baby to Aberdeen, and lived economically on a meagre income.

Fig 3
*Catherine Gordon Byron
by Thomas Stewardson*

Her temper was unpredictable and she often vented her frustrations by shouting at her son. In moments of stress she bawled him out as 'a lame brat'. At times their relationship was very strained particularly regarding money matters – his over-spending and her lack of resources. At other times their relationship verged on affection.

"I hope my son will conduct himself thro' life in a way to do honour to both the great families from which he is descended and that he will be of service to his country. Of his talents there can be no doubt." (Catherine Byron)

"I do believe she likes me, she manifests that in many instances, particularly with regard to money, which I never want and have as much as I desire." (Byron)

Upon her son inheriting Newstead Abbey, Catherine applied to the leader of the House of Lords, to support her application to His Majesty George III for financial assistance.

"By the death of the late Lord Byron that Title devolved upon my son now 12 years of age and with it an estate not exceeding £- a year and that even in a most dilapidated condition. My own situation is simply this: upon my marriage with the late Mr Byron he possessed my fortune which was considerably more than £20,000 but unfortunately for myself and son all that is left is £4,200. I am myself descended from an ancient and noble family, namely Sir Wm. Gordon… It has been mentioned to me that persons in my situation have been thought ye object of His Majesty's bounty."
(Catherine Byron)

She was successful and, with the support of John Hanson (lawyer and business agent), secured £500 p.a. from the Court of Chancery for Byron's education at Harrow School. Whilst at Cambridge University, she gave him all the £500 whilst her pension was reduced to £200 p.a.

"When he does go, an addition allowance must be granted as I intend giving up the £500 to him as I believe he cannot live upon less and before he goes it will take four hundred and fifty pounds for furniture plate and linen, fifty for his wardrobe, and he must have a horse, I suppose which will be fifty more. I am sorry I cannot make him a present of these things … and I am determined not to run into debt." *(Catherine Byron)*

Byron was well impressed with his student grant and claimed to have one of the best allowances in the College.

Nevertheless, Byron's profligacy continued - he purchased three horses instead of one, supported two menservants, purchased a carriage and spent money at will. By the age of eighteen, with the security provided by his widowed landlady Mrs. Massingberd and her daughter, he had entered into an agreement with money-lenders.

It is through his correspondence with his half-sister Augusta Leigh, that we begin to understand the eccentric ups and downs of their relationship. By the time Byron started university in 1805, he perceived her to be his 'tormentor'- whose 'diabolical disposition' increased with age. He claimed that she 'violently' abused him verbally and regularly upbraided him as if he was 'the most undutiful wretch in existence.' It appears that she had refused to accept his claim that their tenant, the twenty-three year old Lord Grey de Ruthyn had made deviant sexual advances to him which he had found abhorrent.

Catherine Byron died of a stroke (aged forty-six) - the day before her son returned home from his foreign travels. News of her imminent demise prompted a quicker return to Newstead than planned. Catherine Gordon Byron was buried at Hucknall Torkard Church in Nottinghamshire. It was the departure of the hearse from Newstead that prompted Byron to write his Will, directing that he should be buried beside his dog Boatswain in the tomb in the garden of Newstead Abbey, without ceremony.

Augusta Maria Byron Leigh (1783- 1851)
Half-sister to Lord George Byron, she married her cousin Lt. Colonel Frederick George Leigh in 1807. The couple had seven children and suitable marriages amongst the children improved their lifestyle in high society and at court. However the marriage did not turn out well. George Leigh enjoyed horse racing and gambled away his money, leaving Augusta and the children little other than his debts. Later in life, the Honourable Augusta Leigh, held the office of Woman of the Bedchamber to Queen Charlotte and continued to occupy apartments in St James's Palace.
Augusta was five years older than Byron and they had not met before he went to Harrow School. Even then, they met only rarely.

From 1804, Augusta wrote to him regularly and became his confidant, especially regarding quarrels with his mother.

''A relation whom I love, a Friend in whom I can confide. In both these lights my Dear Augusta I shall ever look upon you.''
(Byron)

Fig 4
Augusta Mary Leigh
by James Holmes

Their correspondence ceased when Byron embarked on his Mediterranean Tour, but resumed when she sent a letter of condolences on the death of his mother in 1811. The attachment gradually awakened kindred feelings of a more complex nature. Her mild temper and adaptability appealed to Byron. They got on well together and appeared to have fallen in love. When his marriage fell apart and he left England, never to return, rumours of incest were rife. Incest did not challenge the laws of England at the time. It was classed as an ecclesiastical crime of immorality and would therefore have been tried by the Church.

It was widely speculated that her daughter, Elizabeth Medora Leigh, was fathered by Lord Byron, despite the fact that George Leigh was recorded as her legal father.

Augusta Ada King-Noel, Countess of Lovelace (1815-1852)

Lord Byron separated from Annabella Milbanke in 1815, a month after Ada was born. He left England four months later.

Ada was not permitted to know anything about her father or to have access to his poetry or portraits during his lifetime.

Fig 5
Ada King, Countess of Lovelace by Margaret Carpenter

Annabella promoted her daughter's interest in mathematics and logic. Educated at home by private tutors, mathematics became her main subject. Ada worked for some years with Charles Babbage on the Analytical Engine, a predecessor of modern computers. Through their collaboration in the early 1840s, Ada became a pioneer of computer technology, and is recognised as one of the world's first computer programmers.

She married the man she loved, William King, 8th. Lord King and 1st. Earl Lovelace (1805-1893) and they had three children.

When Thomas Wildman purchased Newstead Abbey, Ada visited the ancestral home and spent time reading her father's poetry and letters to friends and his publisher.

Ada was diagnosed with uterine cancer and died at the age of thirty-six. Her last will and testament left instructions that as she had not been allowed to know her father in life, she would rest with him forever in eternity. She was buried beside him inside the Byron vault at Hucknall Torkard Church.

In 1950 a lock-box of some of Ada's possessions was opened and her mathematical notebooks containing her concepts and programme for the first-ever computer algorithms (written in 1843) were discovered. The computer language developed for the US Department of Defense in the early 1980s was named 'Ada' in her honour. In 2024, 'Ada' will be used widely around the world. It is the most commonly used language for mission-critical defence software.

4. PHYSICAL APPEARANCE

4a. Observations by Byron and his Contemporaries

Lameness (and weak right side)

Byron was born with a deformed right foot – commonly referred to by his contemporaries as a club foot. There were several abnormalities apparent – a withered calf, a shorter leg and an inward twisting of the ankle causing him to walk on the side of his foot. At the post-mortem examination, Dr. Meyer (Swiss editor of the Greek Chronicle) commented upon Byron's good looks and the apparent congenital deformity in one foot and leg:

"The only blemish of his body, which otherwise might have vied with Apollo himself was the congenital malformation… The foot was deformed and turned inwards, and the leg was smaller and shorter than the sound one… There can be little or no doubt that he was born club-footed."

The precise cause remains somewhat unclear. At the time, it was sometimes referred to as a withered calf muscle and a club foot caused simply by a twisted achilles tendon.

Fig 6
Lord George Gordon Byron as a child
Steel engraving
by H. Payne

Current thinking may focus more upon congenital talipes equinovarus (talipes from the Latin 'to walk on the ankle').

"It turns inward and he walks quite on the side of his foot."
(Catherine Byron - George aged four)

Byron wore an inner sole and brace during his early school years (St Glennie's School in Dulwich). He did not like wearing a brace. He preferred to wear specially made shoes and long baggy breeches. The fact that he was born with a severe disability in one foot made any form of exercise involving walking or running difficult. Walking even quite short distances outdoors caused him pain as well as the humiliation of not being able to keep up with others. He was especially sensitive about the infirmity and did all he could to conceal it.

Right eye smaller than the left
This difference was recorded both verbally and visually by many observers. In a letter to John Murray, Newton Hanson, the son of Byron's solicitor and schoolmate at Harrow, stated that when Byron arrived there, the boys saw that one of his eyes was visibly larger than the other. The difference in the size was as much as a sixpence and a shilling - so they called him eighteen pence!

There is a lack of consistency in regard to the colour of Byron's eyes – often described as a greyish brown or blueish grey:
"They were of a greyish brown, but of peculiar clearness, and when animated possessed a fire which seemed to look through and penetrate the thoughts of others." (Thomas Medwin)

The only known close up miniature where Byron is showing his smaller right eye. In the 1800s, fashion dictated that he use Macassar oil to strengthen and control his curls.

Fig 7
Watercolour portrait miniature of Lord Byron
by Girolamo Prepiani

Other notable facial features
Pale complexion - an 'alabaster' skin
Small, regular white teeth - reflected a phobia for cleaning his teeth and a vast collection of toothbrushes
Dimpled chin
Large well-shaped nose
Wide range of facial expressions - reflected his extreme mood changes e.g. scornful and indignant; deep habitual thought; melancholy; animated mirth and gaiety

Hair colour and style
This was described in a variety of shades and styles at different life stages -
Darker shades of brown or back; a light chestnut colour
Long or short natural curls
"My hair once black or a rather very dark brown is turned (I know not how but I presume by perpetual perspiration) to a light chestnut." (Byron)

Weight

Byron was preoccupied with his body shape and weight and prone to dramatic slimming regimes. In 2024, Byron would be seen to suffer from Bulimia Nervosa, an eating disorder (and mental health condition).

"He went out to cricket to make himself thinner and then went into the bath to boil off his fat."

Not surprisingly, variations in his body weight resulted in significant changes in his overall appearance.

Less than 10 stone - he appeared emaciated and anorexic: *"Thin as a skeleton; hollow cheeks"* Whilst approaching 15 stone - he appeared obese: *"Unrecognisably fat and bloated"*

His Appearance – as described by close contacts

Thomas Medwin (writer and poet)

"I saw a man of about 5ft 8 inches. His face was fine. His forehead was high and temples broad and he had a plainness in his complexion. His hair waved in natural and graceful curves over his head. His eyes were placed too close to the nose and one was rather smaller than the other. They were a greyish brown and when animated possessed a fire."

Sir Walter Scott (Scottish historian, novelist and poet)

"The predominating expression was that of a deep and habitual thought, which gave way to the most vapid play of features when he engaged in interesting discussion; so that a brother poet compared them to a beautiful alabaster vase, only seen to perfection when lighted up from within. The flashes of mirth, gaiety, indignation, or satirical dislike which frequently animated Lord Byron's countenance might, during an evening's entertainment be mistaken by a stranger for the habitual expression of melancholy."

Appearance Timeline

The mature student

Long rough curly hair; darkish brown curls falling over the forehead
Round chin; Large nose; Full lips and shorter upper lip
Blue grey eyes; Right eye noticeably smaller than left
White teeth
Flexible body; Open chest; Broad beam; Round limbs
'Alabaster' skin and white hands

At 5 feet 8.5 inches and weighing 14 stone 4 pounds - Byron introduced a dramatic slimming regime to reduce his naturally chubby figure- a vegetarian diet combined with activity (running /cricket), hot baths and no alcohol.

Fig 8

Byron in Undergraduate dress c.1806
Anonymous

As a result of the new slimming regime, Byron turned himself from 'a plump little boy with a limp' into 'a strikingly handsome man.'

"I am grown very thin as I found myself too plump. I have now lost 2 stone and a half and weigh 12 stone... my visage is lengthened, I appear taller & somewhat slim... my hair once black or rather very dark brown, is turned to a light chestnut... so that I am metamorphosed not a little." (Byron)

The Dandy

Byron enjoyed dressing up and developed into a dandyfied young aristocrat - with ruffled shirt, high collar, cream trousers and small black shoes. He used the same tailor as his personal friend, Beau Brummell, and was seen to adopt the familiar Beau Brummell facial expressions - the look of studied boredom and the fleeting glance of indifference or disdain. Together they ranked as the two great heart-throbs of the Romantic era.

In 1815, Thomas Moore (Irish writer and poet), recalled his first impressions of Lord Byron after a breakfast party of poets at the home of the poet Samuel Rogers:
"I chiefly remember to have remarked upon the nobleness of his air, His beauty... the pure, spiritual paleness of his features." (Thomas Moore)

A somewhat less flattering opinion was expressed by John Murray's son when he reflected on his recollections of a visit by Lord Byron to see his father at the publisher's house in Albemarle Street, Mayfair in London.
"He appeared to me rather a short man, with a handsome countenance... he wore many rings on his fingers, and a brooch in his shirt front... Lord Byron's deformity in his foot was very evident, especially as he walked downstairs. He carried a stick...

After Scott and he had ended their conversation in the drawing-room, it was a curious sight to see the two great poets of the age - both lame - stumbling downstairs side by side.''(John Murray 3rd)

Iconic Appearance

A manly figure and handsome
A countenance pre-possessing and expressive
A high forehead and broad temples
A pale complexion
Shorter hair waved in a natural and graceful style

''Lord Byron's appearance at that time was the finest I ever saw it. His dress, which was black, with white trousers completed the succinctness and gentlemanliness of his appearance...
He resembled in a lively manner the portrait of him by Phillips, by far the best that has appeared: I mean the best of him at his best time of life, and the most like him in features as well as expression.''(Leigh Hunt - critic, essayist, journalist and poet)

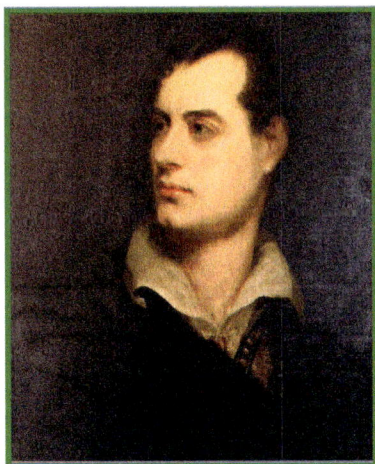

''Taller than average and stunningly handsome. A charming smile and voice. Romantic looking and sexually attractive.'' (Lady Westmoreland's Ball)

Fig 9
George Gordon 6th Baron Byron by Thomas Griffiths Wainewright

The Ageing Poet

"Lord Byron could not have been more than 30, but he looked 40. His face had become pale, bloated and sallow. He had grown very fat, his shoulders broad and round, and the knuckles of his hands were lost in fat. (Newton Hanson 1818)
"My hair is growing grey & my teeth are sometimes looseish though still white and sound. Would not one think I was sixty instead of not quite nine and twenty." (Byron)

Fig 10
George Gordon Noel Byron
by Charles Turner

The Cavalier Servente

Byron's appearance changed dramatically whilst in Genoa with Teresa Guiccioli. On the one hand he was identified as being in his prime:
"He was in the prime of his life, thirty-four, of middle height, regular features, without a strain or furrow on his plaid skin. His shoulders broad, chest open, body and limbs finely proportioned...

His small highly finished head and curly hair had an airy and graceful appearance from the massiveness and length of his throat."
(Edward Trelawny; Biographer and novelist)

Others perceived an altogether older and more decrepit version of his former self:
Emaciated with hollow cheeks and loose teeth
Greying and receding hair
Depressed with little or no interest in his style of dress

"Byron appears distinctly emaciated, and also prematurely aged and stooped for his 33 years. Leaning on his stick and with his hair receding fast from his forehead." (Count Alfred D'Orsay 1822)

"The most famous poet of the age dressed in dingy old clothes far too large for him." (Lady Blessington's diary)

Byron himself was aware of these dramatic changes in his physique and questioned whether they were due to ill-health.

Byron was an accomplished horseman. Seen here in a riding costume holding his riding crop.

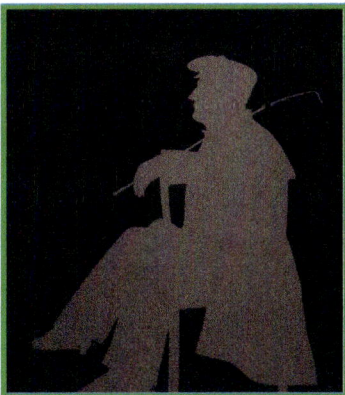

Fig11
*George Gordon Noel Byron
print of a silhouette cut in paper by
Marianne Hunt*

4b. Portraits Busts & Statues

Portraits

Two iconic portraits of Lord Byron spring to mind immediately, each with a very different provenance. They are the oil paintings created by Thomas Phillips RA in 1813-1814:
- Portrait of a Nobleman - commonly referred to as The Cloak
- Portrait of a Nobleman dressed as an Albanian - often referred to simply as The Albanian

The Cloak was commissioned by Byron's publisher, John Murray, in 1813. He proposed using it as an engraving for publishing purposes. Byron made strenuous efforts to control the presentation of his own face and figure in virtually all his portraits.

Newstead Abbey was sold to Thomas Wildman in 1818. At Wildman's request, Byron sent him his portrait by Phillips.

Fig 12
George Gordon, 6th Lord Byron by Thomas Phillips 1813

Byron himself commissioned The Albanian portrait and it was created at the same time he sat for The Cloak. The face (despite the mustachios) is almost identical and he is wearing the same dark brooch in both portraits.

The costume was purchased by Byron on his travels to Epirus in Greece during 1809. He purchased two outfits for 50 guineas and described them as - *"The most magnificent in the world."*

The Albanian portrait was purchased from Thomas Phillips by Byron's mother-in-law Lady Noel, upon the marriage of her daughter Anne Isabella Milbanke to Lord Byron.

Ada received the portrait upon her marriage to Lord Lovelace at the age of nineteen.

Fig 13
Lord Byron in Albanian dress by Thomas Phillips 1813

The portrait remained in the Lovelace family until Ada's great grandson sold it to the Ministry of Works in 1952. It now resides in the British Ambassador's Residence in Athens.

When Byron travelled to Greece to support the War of Independence, he expressed his affinity with Scotland and once again took to wearing his Gordon tartan.

"My heart warms to the Tartan or to anything of Scotland which reminds me of Aberdeen and other parts not so far from the Highlands as that town." (Letter to Sir Walter Scott 1822)

Byron's Scottish ancestry entitled him to wear the Gordon and Royal Stuart tartans. Here he is shown as a war hero in the making. The cavalry helmet he designed himself, based upon descriptions of armour in Homer's Iliad.

Fig 14
*Hand coloured lithograph of Lord Byron
by R.Martin*

Miniatures

Byron enthusiastically endorsed the socal custom of exchanging miniatures and private portraits with close, personal friends. Different miniatures were created based on the work by George Sanders - the Scottish miniaturist and portrait painter.

Fig 15 *After Sanders*

Girolamo Prepiani captured the appeal that military costumes held for Byron. He was seen to wear one of his uniforms whenever a Greek deputation arrived at his residence.
On his arrival in Missolonghi, understanding the importance and symbolism of the moment, he donned his scarlet military costume.

Fig 16 *by Girolamo Prepiani*

Byron was somewhat less enthusiastic about sitting for a bust.
"A picture is a different matter - everybody sits for their picture - but a bust looks like putting up pretensions to permanency and smacks something of a hankering for public fame rather than private remembrance." (Byron)

Busts and Statues

Fig 17
Bust of Lord Byron
by Edward Hodges Baily RA c1826

The white marble bust by
Thorvaldsen, modelled for
John Cam Hobhouse.

Fig 18
George Gordon Byron
Carved Bust
by Bertel Thorvaldsen (Rome 1817)

We can only surmise what Lord Byron would have thought of his
statue in the Wren Library at his alma mater, and the many
monuments to be found around the globe in 2024.

Missolonghi: The Byron Society

Athens: The Zappeion Garden

Missolonghi Garden of heroes

Byron was well known for his attempts to manipulate his image through the way he was presented in his portraits. What would he have done in 2024 with Adobe Photoshop!

'A riddle wrapped in a mystery inside an enigma'
April 2024

5. CHARACTER AND PERSONALITY TRAITS

5a. Childhood and Adolescence

Early Childhood
A self-conscious young boy regarding his deformities. At times he felt ugly, deformed and an outcast.
He suffered an innate and paralysing shyness and sensitivity.
He was a boy of solitude – subdued and withdrawn.
He was under the control of a schizophrenic mother and an abusive nurse who addressed him as "a fatherless lame brat."

After George was breached, he wore skeleton suits, with tight long trousers and a short jacket and a large, open ruffled collar. In line with the fashion of the day, he wore his hair long at shoulder length.

Fig 19
Lord Byron at the age of seven
Engraving by Edward Finden after
watercolour by William Kay 1795

Harrow and Southwell 1803-8
He felt himself to be an outsider due to his deformity and inherent shyness.
He got into a number of fights with other students (but allegedly, he only lost one!).

He preferred sports that required hard physical strength such as boxing and swimming.

Byron did not look forward to the school holidays at home in Southwell with his mother.

"She is so hasty, so impatient, that I dread the approach of the holidays, more than most boys do their return from them."(Byron - Letter to Augusta 1804)

Newstead, with its close proximity to Annesley Hall, proved the ideal base to visit his adolescent love, Mary Chaworth.

Fig 20
Byron amongst the ruins at Newstead

At the age of sixteen his aspirations were high:
"I will cut myself a path through the world or perish in the attempt... I will carve myself the passage to Grandeur but never with Dishonour." (Byron - Letter to Catherine Byron 1804)

His mother however had cause for concern:
"What is to be done with him when he leaves Harrow god only knows. He is a turbulent unruly boy that wants to be emancipated from all restraint, his sentiments are however noble."(Catherine Byron)

University 1805-1808

He was seen as a strikingly handsome, self-respecting aristocrat.
His 'super-excellent rooms' were located in the Great Court.

Fig 21
Lord Byron when at Cambridge
Watercolour drawing
by Gilchrist

Initially Byron struggled to settle into university life. The move toward a very different life stage proved somewhat frightening - *"to feel that I was no longer a boy."*

The college authorities had told him that dogs were banned and that he could not bring his pet bulldog. Annoyed by this, he bought Bruin the Bear and installed him in the tower above his rooms. He even suggested he would apply for a college fellowship for Bruin!

He started to spend money well beyond his means:
new furniture, china and crystal, a large four poster bed
a variety of alcoholic beverages: wine, port, claret and madeira
He was meticulous about cleanliness:
obsessed with cleaning his teeth and taking a warm bath every day
(after his daily swim)
His chameleon character became even more clearly apparent:
withdrawn, silent, depressed, vivacious, happy, witty, flippant

Discovering politics at University, Byron was inclined to liberalism
and joined up with John Cam Hobhouse - the founder of The Whig
Club and 'Amicable Society'. His opinions were those of an
intelligent intellectual and a political revolutionary.

He graduated with an MA. As a nobleman, he was not asked to
attend lectures or take public exams.

Newstead Abbey (1808 - 1814)

George Gordon
Byron inherited
Newstead Abbey at
the age of ten.

Fig 22
*West view of Newstead
Abbey*

Byron returned to Newstead Abbey after university.

Whilst at Newstead, Byron showed a range of appealing traits:
He was kind - a feeling heart; no malice
He treated servants with genuine affection - feeling protective and responsible
He was indulgent toward his animals- dogs, cats, horses and his bear

Throughout his life, Byron considered dogs to be his best friends. His *Epitaph to a Dog* is immortalised on Boatswain's tomb at Newstead Abbey.

Fig 23
Lord Byron and his favourite
Popular Portrait Gallery

When some proud Son of Man returns to Earth,
Unknown to Glory but upheld by Birth,
The sculptor's art exausts the pomp of woe,
And storied urns record who rests below:
When all is done, upon the Tomb is seen
Not what he was, but what he should have been.
But the poor Dog, in life the firmest friend,
The first to welcome, foremost to defend,
Whose honest heart is still his Masters own,
Who labours, fights, lives, breathes for him alone,
Unhonour'd falls, unnotic'd all his worth,
Deny'd in heaven the Soul he held on earth:
While man, vain insect! hopes to be forgiven,
And claims himself a sole exclusive heaven,
Oh man! thou feeble tenant of an hour,
Debas'd by slavery, or corrupt by power,
Who knows thee well, must quit thee with disgust,
Degraded mass of animated dust!
Thy love is lust, thy friendship all a cheat,
Thy tongue hypocrisy, thy heart deceit,
By nature vile, ennobled but by name,
Each kindred brute might bid thee blush for shame.
Ye! who behold perchance this simple urn,
Pass on, it honours none you wish to mourn,
To mark a friend's remain these stones arise,
I never know but one - and here he lies.

Fig 24 *Portrait of Boatswain by Clifton Tomson*

Fig 25 *Boatswain's marble funerary monument at Newstead Abbey*

The sections above Byron's poem are a memorial to Boatswain and an introduction to the poem, written by John Cam Hobhouse:

"Near this Spot are deposited the Remains of one who possessed Beauty without Vanity, Strength without Insolence, Courage without Ferosity, and all the virtues of Man without his Vices.
This praise, which would be unmeaning Flattery if inscribed over human Ashes, is but a just tribute to the Memory of BOATSWAIN, a DOG"

5b. Adulthood

A capricious and chameleon-like character
High expectations of himself
A fundamental need to be perfect
A Man of Vision & Worshipper of the ideal

At one end of the spectrum he was seen as:
Gentlemanly
Happy vivacious and gay
Genial and good-humoured
Animated and cheerful when speaking
Highly energetic: spirited; lively; sense of energy
Humorous witty and flippant; hilariously funny and droll
Warm hearted and kind
Generous: gave money to the poor; paid for the education of staff
Kind and affectionate - particularly toward servants and animals

Educated and intelligent; shrewd and astute
Deep thinking - an introspective approach to problem-solving
A perfectionist with a fear of negative judgement

Sitting in Quiet Contemplation
A Romantic Dreamer
or
A deep thinking Ruminator

Fig 26
Lord Byron
by Richard Westall

His deep thinking sometimes became overthinking - and led to stress, anxiety and depression.

Thomas Moore, on their first meeting in 1811, observed:

'The gentleness of his voice and manners… when he spoke, there was a perpetual play of lively thought, though melancholy was their habitual character, when in repose.'' (Thomas Moore)

"His beauty drew every eye upon him when he entered a room. No picture is like him… In talents he was unequalled and his faults were those rather of a bizarre temper arising from an eager and irritable nervous habit than any depravity of disposition. He was devoid of selfishness. He was generous, humane and noble-minded when passion did not blind him.'' (Sir Walter Scott)

At times he was:

Intolerant, blunt and obnoxious - he did not suffer fools gladly

Arrogant, haughty, contemptuous and 'a bit of a snob'

Unfeeling and cruel - with a vicious acerbic wit

Some of the expressions Byron adopted in his portraits were seen to reinforce these observations. Others perceived the raised chin and disdainful look to be a matter of poetic licence.

Fig 27
*Engraving by Henry Meyer c.1815
After painting by George Henry Harlow*

At the other end of the spectrum he was extremely sensitive and quick to take offence

Potentially violent in his response to criticism or insult

Tempestuous and prone to violent mood swings

Susceptible to bursts of anger - especially when frustrated or thwarted and unable to achieve his desires
Susceptible to rages and black moods; destructive

At other times he was:
Cold silent and reserved; subdued and withdrawn
Grave, brooding, gloomy, despondent, despairing
Prone to deep-seated melancholy and depression
Introverted; reserved and shy

A loner and a hermit: he sought solitude; enjoyed time alone; well able to amuse himself
"I only go out in society to get me a fresh appetite for being alone."
"I do not know that I am happiest when alone; but this I am sure of, that I never am long in society, even of her I love, without a yearning for the company of my lamp and my utterly confused and tumbled-over library." (Byron)

In 2024, Byron's behaviour would suggest:
Bipolar - mood swings with episodes of extreme highs and lows
Severe episodes of mania or depression, bordering on psychosis
Paralysingly self-conscious and Social-phobic - anxiety, inhibitions and fear of interacting with strangers (especially at public events)
Bulimia- preoccupied with weight and body shape

In the modern healthcare context, Byron may also have been considered a 'Misophoniac'. Misophonia is a selective sound sensitivity disorder whereby individuals suffer a reflexive response of extreme anger to certain, specific noises which are made by other people. The most common trigger is noisy eating. In Misophoniacs, the response to the key sounds by-passes the rational areas of the brain and instead, is hard-wired into the fight or flight area. This can result in extreme agitation, anger and rage.

6. INTERESTS, PURSUITS & PLEASURES

Whilst at Harrow School, Byron excelled in oratory, wrote verse and played sports.

By the age of nineteen, he showed an interest in:

History, Greek and Latin literature, Biographies, Poetry, Philosophy and Law.

He was a keen sportsman who participated in a wide variety of activities:

Boxing – taught by John Gentleman Jackson; Professor of Pugilism and Boxing Champion of England

Pistol shooting - self-taught

Fencing – taught by Henry Angelo: using foils, single sticks and broadsword

Horse riding

Cricket

Swimming -

England - Newstead Upper Lake; The Cam (Cambridge) in competition with Edward Long; The Thames

Once abroad - The Tagus River from Lisbon to Belem Castle; from The Lido to the Grand Canal; Crossing the Hellespont (Dardanelles) from Sestos to Abydos

''I was an excellent swimmer - a decent though not at all a dashing rider & was sufficient of fence - particularly of the Highland broadsword… not a bad boxer - when I could keep my temper and I was besides a very fair cricketer - one of Harrow Eleven when we play against Eton in 1805.'' (Byron)

"There are three things I can do which you cannot. I can swim across that river - I can snuff out that candle at the distance of twenty paces and I have written a poem of which fourteen thousand copies were sold in a day." (Byron in conversation with Dr John Polidori)

He exhibited a fervent love of animals and nature
He cared deeply for his own dogs, horses and any injured animals or birds, in need of assistance
Anti fishing, hunting, shooting

Byron was an avid and retentive reader of books. He possessed an ever expanding Library. His interests were often focussed upon: history, the classics and antiquity
Literature and philosophy: He spent time in discussion with leading literary figures at John Murray's publishing house at 50 Albemarle Street, Mayfair, London
Languages: He spoke six other languages - Latin, Greek, French, Italian, German and some Armenian

Theatre: He was initially attracted to the theatre during his school holidays in Southwell. Whilst living in London in his twenties, he often attended Drury Lane and later became their chief literary adviser.

Byron enjoyed socialising with close friends - drinking at the Cocoa Tree Club (St. James Street) and at Newstead Abbey where they sometimes dressed up as cannons and drank from a skull cup.

He enjoyed dressing in a flamboyant and dandyfied manner. He was known for his dash and panache and love of fancy dress - especially exotic cloaks and turbans.

He longed for new and exciting sensations:
"The great object of life is sensation – to feel that we exist, even though, in pain."(Byron - Letter to Annabella 1813)

Dislikes
Attending social occasions and meeting strangers. Aside from being introverted and social-phobic, he found dancing with a club foot virtually impossible. The Waltz and the Quadrille were the dances of preference during the 1820s.

Mounting debts proved to be a constant concern up until the sale of Newstead Abbey in 1818. His debts amounted to c.£34,000 when he sold the property to Thomas Wildman for £94,500.
Clearly, Byron had never learnt responsible estate management.

"Mismanagement is the hereditary epidemic of (the Byron) brood."
(Byron)

7. POLITICS, WAR & RELIGION

Byron Coat of Arms:

Two wild maned and energetic chestnut horses surmounted by a mermaid with comb and mirror.   The motto **Crede Byron** (Trust Byron).

Fig 28
The Newstead Abbey Byron Society

Politics

Having discovered politics at University, Byron was inclined to liberalism. He identified with the suppressed minority and was committed to freedom of the individual. He was aptly described as a Liberal Whig, a Political Rebel and Intellectual Revolutionary.

His maiden speech in the House of Lords was on February 27th. 1812 – a plea opposing harsh Tory measures against riotous Nottingham weavers. The Frame Breakers Act applied the death penalty for Luddites convicted of destroying the new machinery that was causing unemployment and starvation.

"Suppose, my lord, Your Bill made law,
Regard the prisoner brought up for judgement, dull with misery,
Weak with starvation, weary of a life.
That by your reckoning is of less account
Than one dismantled loom.
Regard this man
Torn from the family whose breadwinner
He may not be (although the will is there),
Dragged into court.

Who will pronounce the verdict?
Twelve honest men and true?
Never, my lords!
Command twelve butchers as your jury-men,
And make a hangman Judge!''

''The best speech I have ever heard by a Lord since the 'Lord knows when.'' (Radical leader Sir Francis Burdett)

At the next hearing, the death penalty was replaced with 14 years transportation.

Byron's next speech was during the Roman Catholic Debate on April 21st 1812. He supported the proposal, extending civil rights to Roman Catholics, who had been excluded from participating in public life.
"Challenging the inequitable system that makes one set of rules for the common man another set of rules for the aristocracy." (Byron)

In 1814 he was approached by a man in a Debtor's prison and asked to present a petition to The Lords on behalf of inmates. Byron declined and showed no more interest in attending the House of Lords.
"They told me that my manner of speaking was not dignified enough for the Lords, but was more calculated for the Commons. I believe it was a Don Juan kind of speech. The two occasions were, the Catholic Question and some Manufacturing affair." (Thomas Medwin - Conversations of Lord Byron)

His most notable political opponents were identified as -
The Duke of Wellington - Tory Prime Minister and one of the Commanders who defeated Napoleon at the Battle of Waterloo:
''The best of the Cut-throats''

Lord Castlereagh - Foreign Secretary and Leader of the House of Commons: "The Intellectual Eunuch"

Freedom Fighter and Political Statesman

Byron disliked wars in principle and on the eve of Waterloo, whilst at the Duchess of Richmond's Ball, he defined war as *"a contemplation of the futility of bravery and the bloodshed in purposeless slaughter."*

In particular he despised wars of aggression waged for personal gain and championed those conflicts that defended freedom. In later life, he was a member of the Italian Carbonari – a secret society dedicated to Italian unity and driving out the Austrians. In 1823 he advocated Greek Independence from the Ottoman Empire.

Anti-monarchy

George lll was King of Great Britain and Ireland from 1760 to 1820 (he died at the age of eighty-one). He was also a monarch of the House of Hanover. He married Princess Charlotte of Mecklenburg-Strelitz with whom he had fifteen children including Prince Augustus Frederick, Duke of Sussex. He is the longest-lived and longest-reigning male monarch. He was largely considered to be an ineffectual king at this late stage – blind and mad.

John Hunt was indicted for libel as publisher of Byron's *The Vision of Judgement*. It defamed the previously favourable reputations of George III and the Prince Regent and thus brought the monarchy into disrepute.

Initially Byron expressed great admiration for Napoleon Bonaparte, but was subsequently disillusioned by the widespread savagery of The Napoleonic Wars. He wrote an *Ode to Napoleon* upon his abdication and exile to Elba – an ode of both grief and reproach.

Religion

Brought up to be a staunch Calvinist, Byron tended towards a dislike of Reformed Christianity and its emphasis upon the sovereignty of God. He did, however, believe in God.

"I do not go to church, like many of my accusers; but I have my hopes I am not less a Christian than they for God examines the inward part of the man, not outward appearance." (William Fletcher conversation with Byron; letter to Dr Kennedy May 1824)

Nanny Smith recalled how Lord Byron was frequently seen reading the Bible. She had taken note of the verse on the fly-leaf of his Bible.

> *"Within this sacred volume lies*
> *The mystery of all mysteries*
> *Oh! happy he of human race*
> *To whom our God hath given grace*
> *To read, to learn, to watch, to pray,*
> *To lift the latch, to form the way,*
> *But better he had ne'er been born,*
> *Who reads to doubt, who reads to scorn."*

He sent his daughter Allegra to a Catholic convent in Romagna, Italy. Byron's valet William Fletcher, recalled hearing Byron quote from the Bible during his final days.

"Had my lord not been a Christian, this book (Byron's bible) would most naturally have been thrown aside, and of course he would have been ignorant of so many fine passages which I have heard him repeat at intervals, when in the midst of his last fatal illness. (William Fletcher Letter to Dr Kennedy; Zante May 1824)

Lord Byron's beliefs would most accurately be categorised as Deism. Deism originated in Europe, mainly amongst intellectuals. It asserted that God exists, but does not intervene in the functioning of the natural world.

8. THE GRAND TOUR 1809-1811

The Grand Tour was a trip around Continental Europe that young men took after finishing college. Byron's tour was focused on the Mediterranean due to the Napoleonic Wars.

Fig 29
George Gordon, 6th Lord Byron
by George Sanders
Commissioned by Byron in 1807

Byron had a passionate longing to see exotic lands which he had cherished since boyhood. This longing was intensified by the need to break away from his own indiscretions and motivated by his secret love for Mary Chaworth - her rejection and his jealousy of her husband, John Musters.
"I never will be in England if I can avoid it, why - must remain a secret." (Byron)

He was besieged by creditors, but nevertheless he continued to spend money on books and miniature portraits of himself and friends in anticipation of his departure.

Aged twenty one, Byron finally raised the necessary capital (including £4,600 lent to him by his friend Scrope Davies - from the profits of his gambling). Along with John Cam Hobhouse and servants including Joe Murray, William Fletcher and his page Robert Rushton, he travelled to Falmouth to take passage on the Princess Elizabeth on July 2nd 1809.

PORTUGAL: Lisbon - Byron was very taken with Cintra and swam the Tagus across to Belem (just over one mile).
SPAIN: Seville and then Cadiz - where Byron attended a bullfight.
GIBRALTAR: Byron expressed little interest in Gibraltar. At that time Britain and Spain were allied against Napoleon.
"I have just arrived at this place after a journey through Portugal and a part of Spain of nearly 500 miles. We left Lisbon and travelled on horseback to Seville and Cadiz and then in the Hyperion frigate to Gibraltar." (Byron)
Robert Rushton (in poor health) was sent back to England from Gibraltar. Byron was concerned that the Ottoman Empire might have proved unsafe for his young page. He paid for Robert's education and requested that his mother be kind to the lad.
SARDINIA: Cagliari - Byron was presented to his majesty Victor Emmanuel I.
"My next stage is Cagliari in Sardinia where I shall be presented to his majesty. I have a most superb uniform (as a court dress), Indispensable in travelling." (Byron)
MALTA: Byron was diverted by Spyridon Forresti (British Consul of Corfu) to take the Royal Navy escort vessel to the gulf of Patras and Preveza in Western Greece and then to travel on to visit Ali Pasha in Ioannina (Albania). He was thus commissioned to visit Ali Pasha on behalf of Naval and Diplomatic Intelligence and as an Official envoy of his Majesty.

IOANNINA: The Pashalik was autonomous within the Ottoman Empire. It covered large areas of South Albania, North-west Greece and North Macedonia. Ali Pasha was one of the most powerful men in the Ottoman Empire - controlling Albania and Epirus while the Morea (Peloponnese peninsula) was ruled by his son Veli Pasha. Ali Pasha was not in residence upon Byron's arrival. He had decreed that Byron was his personal guest and that there should be no expense spared to entertain him and John Cam Hobhouse.

"When I reached Yanina, the capital, I found that Ali Pacha was with his army in Illyricum, besieging Ibrahim Pacha... He had... left orders in Yanina, with the commandant to provide a house, and supply me - with every kind of necessary gratis."(Byron - Letter to Catherine Byron)

Byron spent his free time writing the long poem that would become known as *Childe Harold's Pilgrimage* - the travels of a disaffected youthful aristocrat hero.

GREECE: Byron's first sight of Greece was the Gulf of Lepanto and Missolonghi (under Turkish control).

Heading for Patras, a shipwreck meant Byron came ashore at Souli. This resulted in a long term admiration for the Souliotes - a mountain people who spoke Greek and dressed in the Albanian manner. They were recognised as ferocious fighters.

Byron travelled on to Loutraki, Missolonghi, Patras, Vostitsa (Algio) and the port of Itea.

This was followed by a visit to the ancient sanctuary of Delphi, Parnassos, Thebes - and finally, Athens. At this time Athens was a walled town of some 12,000 inhabitants with a natural fortress - The Acropolis. There was a small mosque inside the Temple of Athena at the Parthenon. Here Byron embarked on canto 2 of *Childe Harold - "Abode of Gods whose shrines no longer burn."*

Lord Elgin had left Athens seven years earlier, in January 1803. Stanzas of *Childe Harold* deplored Elgin's violation of the Acropolis.
"Yet they should violate each saddening shrine
  And bear these altars o'er the long reluctant brine."
"I opposed and will ever oppose, the robbery of ruins from Athens to instruct English in sculpture." (Byron)

Byron lodged at the home of the widow Makri on the corner of Agios Theklas and Papanikolis Street. He flirted with all three daughters, but It was to the twelve year old Theresa that he addressed the poem *'Maid of Athens; ere we part.'*

"I had almost forgotten to tell you that I am dying for love of three Greek girls at Athens, sisters - Teresa, Mariana, and Katinea are the names of these divinities."(Byron - Letter to Henry Drury; Master at Harrow School)

TURKEY: Smyrna and the Ancient city of Ephesus. In Troy, Byron swam each night. He swam around five kilometres across the Hellespont (Dardanelles) from Sestos to Abydos in 1 hour and 10 minutes. Byron imitated Ovid's Leander, who swam every night across the water from Europe to Asia, to reach his love Hero. One night, halfway through the swim, in a strong winter wind, Leander lost his way and drowned.

"I plume myself on this achievement more than I could possibly do on any kind of glory, political, poetical or rhetorical." (Byron)
"This morning I swam from Sestos to Abydos, the immediate distance is not above a mile but the current renders it hazardous, so much so, that I doubt whether Leander's conjugal powers must not have been exhausted in his passage to paradise." (Byron - letter to Henry Drury, Master at Harrow School; May 1810)

His final destination before leaving Turkey was Constantinople where he attended an audience with Sultan Mahmoud II. After visiting Constantinople, Byron and Hobhouse parted company.

John Cam Hobhouse returned to England and Byron proceeded to
Zea and then back to Athens.
*"The further I proceed from your country (England) the less I regret
leaving it... I would be a citizen of the world." (Byron)*
GREECE: Byron stayed at the Capuchin Monastery, where he studied
Italian and Modern Greek with the help of Nicolo Girauld - a student
c. fourteen/ fifteen years of age. It was here that Byron wrote *Hints
of Horace*.

The interior of the
monument was six feet in
diameter and served as a
library and study.

Fig 30
*Interior view of the Lysicrates
monument
Engraving by Charles Heath
from a drawing by S.Pompardi*

It was Nicolo who took on the role of Major Domo when Byron set
off on a visit to the Peloponnese. They visited Olympia where Byron
was seriously ill with a fever (most likely malaria). They parted
company in Malta.
Byron, by his own admission, had caught gonorrhoea in Athens.
He was treated in Malta in 1811 by Surgeon Tucker.

As a result of his Grand Tour, Byron experienced at first hand the
wonders of Greece and roots of Western civilisation. Such events
were likely to have impacted strongly upon his future life as a great
poet, freedom-fighter and statesman of a new age.

9. RETURNING TO ENGLAND AND THE BURDEN OF DEBT

Byron was strapped for cash throughout his travels. John Hanson (Byron's Lawyer and Business agent), failing to resolve issues and settle affairs, suggested selling Newstead Abbey. By this time four bailiffs were in the house. Writing to his mother, he emphatically stated his refusal to sell. In her letter she replied to him:
"I am glad you have refused to sell Newstead, stick to that, stick to it, but this I need not urge knowing your firmness, but dearest Byron if you are unfortunate it will bring down my grey hairs with sorrow to the grave. You are not yet ruined, or much injured, if you take care in future of what you are about." (Catherine Byron 1811)

Concerned about his debts he wrote again to John Hanson who still felt strongly that Newstead Abbey should be sold. Byron again refused.
"Two years travel has tolerably seasoned me to privations … Newstead is out of the question." (Byron)

On reaching London, Byron made an effort to reassure his creditors.

He then made the decision to base himself at Newstead Abbey for the foreseeable future.

Fig 31
*West View of Newstead Abbey
by Peter Tillemans*

A Tour of Byron's Newstead Abbey

Byron lived at Newstead Abbey (on and off) between c.1808 and 1814. Limited funds were available, and there was only sufficient money to furnish a few rooms in the house. The rest were left close to ruin. I have based this section largely on the opinions held by Rosalys Coope and Peter Smith in 2014. It is apparent however, that they too, found it difficult to identify the exact location of certain rooms and the furnishings they contained during Byron's time there.

The contents of the Great Hall had been sold off by the 5th. Lord Byron. The Poet used it (along with his friends), for pistol shooting. On occasion, it was inhabited by Wooly (wolf dog) and Bruin (bear). *"Ascend then, with me the hall steps, that I may introduce you to my Lord and his visitants. But have a care how you proceed; be mindful to go there in broad daylight, and with your eyes about you. For, should you make any blunder, - should you go to the right on the hall steps, you are laid hold of by a bear; and should you go to the left, your case is still worse for you run full against a wolf. If you enter without giving loud notice of your approach, you have only escaped the wolf and the bear to expire by the pistol-shots of the merry Monks of Newstead.(Charles Skinner Mathews Esq. May 1809)*

The Prior's Parlour became a 'scarlet' withdrawing room.

The Prior's Parlour was thus converted into a small dining room where Byron ate all alone or with a few close friends.
Behind the dining room was the 'red withdrawing room'. It seems likely that this was a state room and bedroom for special visitors.

At the top of a spiral staircase were 'three sleeping rooms.' Firstly, the sparsely furnished open space (most probably) occupied by Byron's page Robert Rushton. Proximity to his master ensured that Rushton was always on duty and at Byron's disposal. Byron's dressing room, previously referred to as the Prior's Oratory, was known to be haunted. On the eve of Byron's wedding, the Black Friar warned him that his marriage would be a disaster.

Byron's bedroom had a *'superb 5ft6 bed'* and a lovely view of the lake, the waterfall and Sherwood Forest.

Charles II and Edward III rooms were repaired. At the furthest point away from his own bedroom, was located his mother's bedroom, dressing room and private dining room.

His own library / study overlooked the garden and was located between the dressing room and the pink room. It was here that Byron's bookcases were first located. By 1815, Byron had removed (nearly all) his books from Newstead - some he kept; others were sold.

Byron's drawing room contained some of the furniture that he had brought back from University. Paintings were hung liberally on the walls.

Opinions do differ as to whether it was the drawing room or the study/library that overlooked the Monks Garden and Boatswain's tomb. Previously known as a withdrawing room, the drawing room was typically a room where Byron's visitors were entertained.

The Great Dining Room was no longer in use. Byron and friends used it for their own enjoyment and entertainment.
On the floor below, the Priory Warming Room housed the wine cellar, and it was here that Byron and friends dressed up as cannons and drank from the Skull Cup.
''For the amusements of the morning there was reading, fencing, single-sticks or shuttle-cock in the great room - practising with pistols in the hall - playing with the bear or teazing the wolf. Between seven and eight we dined and our evening lasted from that time till one, two or three in the morning. I must not omit the custom of handing round a human skull filled with burgundy.''(Letter from Charles Skinner Mathews Esq. dated May 1809)

The Chapel was not in use. The monastic slype (passage) was turned into a plunge bath. Ancient Greeks had used cold water bathing as a means of treating fever and for pain relief.

10. SNAPSHOTS OF THE PHASES OF ADULTHOOD

Exciting New Sensations on his Mediterranean Travels
Felt more Relaxed   Sexually and Spiritually free
Persona better suited to European Customs and Conventions
Poetry more widely accepted & Poetic Hero status attained

"The great object of life is sensation -
to feel that we exist, even though, in pain."

A political Liberal A radical Whig & A Champion of the People
Genius of Poetry and Autobiographical Emperor of Words
A Famous Celebrity & Female Heartthrob
Associated with High levels of Social Anxiety

"I awoke one morning and found myself famous."
"A drop of ink may make a million think."

Self-Exile
Notoriety in his home country
Isolated & Alienated by Hardening Public Attitudes

Accusations of illegal or unacceptable Sexual Behaviour
Bi-sexuality   Incest   A Broken Marriage
Desire to protect the Reputation of his half-sister

Radical Politics & Anti-monarchical Stance
Mounting Debts

"You can hardly have forgotten the circumstances under which I
quitted England, nor the rumours of which I was the subject - If they
were true I was unfit for England; if false England is unfit for me."

European Cultural Celebrity of the Modern Age
Prolific Writer of Sensational Works
A Seductive Libertine & A Sexual Braggart

The Philanderer Transformed
Cavalier Servente and Devoted Lover

"Love will find a way through paths where wolves fear to prey."

More Politically Motivated
A Staunch Nationalist & Freedom Fighter

"The 'Byronic hero' must be shorn of his weirdness, and his
self-destructive impulses, and reinvented as a fighter."

More Introverted and Serious in Genoa
Feeling he had Aged Prematurely
Concerned about his Lasting Reputation & Destiny
Turned his back on 'Poeshie'

"I am tired of scribbling, and nothing but the convenience
of an occasional extra thousand pounds
would have induced me to go on."

Seeking a Sense of Higher Purpose
Moving toward a New Course of Action
To invest his Reputation and Money in Greek Independence
The Regeneration of a Nation with a Viable Government

"Think of all the great things that Greece has given the world -
democracy, philosophy, drama, science, medicine ...
and what has the world given back to Greece."

Iconic Philhellene with a Modernist perspective
An Idealist
Birth of a New Age Statesman
Investment in The Greek Cause

"The best way to predict the future is to create it."
'The poet laid down his pen – and donned the warrior's plume"

Failure and Realisation
Unworkable and Unattainable Goals
Mediating amongst Greek Factions Impossible
Founding an Established Order Unlikely

"The great Powers of Europe, will be persuaded
that Greeks are not now capable of governing themselves
and will arrange some means for putting an end to your disorder
which will cut short all your most noble hopes."

Final Transformation into A New Age Statesman
Commitment to The Modernist Movement
Hero of the Greek War of Independence
Martyr to the Cause of Liberty

"I shall probably be obliged to join one of the factions -
which I have hitherto strenuously avoided in the hope
to unite them in one common interest."

The Posthumous Saviour of Greece
Eternal Symbol of Sacrifice for Freedom

"If your reputation as an artist dissipates,
Your memories a champion of Greek freedom will be eternal."

11. POETIC GENIUS AND EMPEROR OF WORDS

11a. Background
Byron's poetry reflected his understanding of the power of language. He stood for freedom of expression and was intolerant of censure by his publishers.
"He was undoubtedly the greatest poetic genius of our century."
(Goethe)

His formula was semi-autobiographical cf. *Childe Harold's Pilgrimage*. A self-declared 'chameleon' poet - he also adopted a comic, satirical tongue in cheek style of writing (cf. *Beppo, The Vision of Judgement* and *Don Juan*). His poetry was sometimes offensive to others, notably his contemptuous abuse of contemporary writers and his monarchical quips regarding Mad King George III.

Initially, Byron would not accept payment for his work. He felt that this would damage his image and social standing. The money went to his literary agent, Robert Dallas. Concerned about his mounting debts, his attitude changed in 1814.

The home and office of his publisher John Murray, 50 Albemarle Street, Mayfair was the centre of a literary circle which included Jane Austen and Sir Walter Scott. It was here that Byron first met Walter Scott. Jane Austen and Byron never met.
"I have read all Walter Scott's novels at least fifty times – wonderful man. I long to get drunk with him."(Byron)

John Murray was always concerned about Byron's controversial views regarding politics, religion and sex, being expressed. This hit a peak during discussions regarding the publication of *Don Juan*:
"I declare to you these were so outrageous that I would not publish them if you would give me your estate."(John Murray 1819)

It was not uncommon for Murray to delay publication or fail to answer letters - often in the hope that Byron would be prepared to reconsider certain text. Conversely, Byron sometimes sought to make changes later on, but resented any delay in publishing his works.

"All the bullies on earth shall not prevent me from writing what I like and publishing what I write." (Byron)

There were times when Byron felt like giving up writing.
"Writing comes over to me in a kind of rage every now and then. If I don't write to empty my mind, I go mad. As to that regular uninterrupted love of writing… I do not understand it. I feel it as a torture, which I must get rid of, and never as a pleasure." (Byron 1821)

Byron has been compared to a wide variety of poets and writers. Along with his contemporary, the German writer Johann Wolfgang von Goethe (1749-1832), he reached the top of the literary charts. Each held the other in high esteem - but never met.

11b. A Small Selection of Byron's Works

Fugitive Pieces
Fugitive Pieces was published privately by George Byron in 1806, when he was eighteen years of age. Some poems had been written whilst at Harrow School when Byron was only fourteen years of age. Others were written during the school holidays in Southwell, Nottinghamshire where Byron resided with his mother. The books were recalled and burnt, on the advice of Rev. John Thomas Becher of Southwell (prebendary of Southwell Minster). He protested that one of the love poems was indecent. Only four copies of Fugitive Pieces remain. The edition was revised and privately published

again in 1807 as **Poems on Various Occasions.** The only public publication of these works appeared in **Hours of Idleness.**

English Bards and Scotch Reviewers

This was a satirical poem that reflected Byron's strong criticism of certain poets, including 'the reigning poets of Romanticism' - namely The Lakeland poets. It targeted a number of notable contemporaries, including William Wordsworth, Robert Southey and Samuel Taylor Coleridge. Although they viewed it as offensive and abusive, it sold well. It established Byron's credentials as a contemporary poet.

Childe Harold's Pilgrimage Cantos 1 & 2

A semi-autobiographical piece, started in Ioannina during Byron's visit to see Ali Pasha in October 1809. It proved to be a long narrative poem in four parts. It described the travels and reflections of a world-weary and disillusioned young man - a young aristocrat travelling to faraway lands filled with sun, romance and war.

The first two cantos of *Childe Harold's Pilgrimage* described Byron's travels through Portugal, Spain, the Ionian Islands and Albania. Once published, Byron achieved Celebrity status.

Fig 32
Childe Harold's Pilgrimage.
Coloured engraving of an 1850 edition

In *Childe Harold*, Byron popularised a new Romantic character type which subsequently manifested itself in most of his heroes. Harold was the first 'Byronic Hero'. The *Childe Harold* travelogue captured the essence of Byron's Mediterranean and Eastern Tour combined with his reflections on the chaos caused by the Napoleonic Wars.

The First Edition of *Childe Harold's Pilgrimage* cantos 1 and 2 (500 quarto copies) was published at the beginning of March 1812 and sold out in three days. It prompted Byron to proclaim - *"I awoke one morning and found myself famous."*
"A poem of most extraordinary power which may rank its author with our first poets." (Sir Walter Scott)

Turkish Tales (1813 – 1816)
The Giaour, The Bride of Abydos, The Corsair
These were Byron's 'Oriental Romances' and the following characteristics were often apparent:
- The hero was depicted as a victim of past or present wrongs
- Heroes had the power to re-invent or transform themselves e.g. *The Giaour* - a Venetian nobleman who transformed himself into an Albanian style fighter
- Heroes were self-destructive and refused redemption e.g. *The Giaour* who banished himself to a monastery, full of remorse

Forbidden love proved to be a common theme.

The Giaour
Leila, one of Hassan's harem, had fallen in love with the Giaour, and was subsequently killed by her Turkish lord. She was thrown into the sea in a sack and left to drown. 'Giaour' is a Turkish word for infidel.

The Giaour avenged Leila's death by killing Lord Hassan.

Fig 33
The Giaour
by Eugene Delacroix 1826

Don Juan (1819-1824)

A satirical epic poem in 16 cantos which portrayed the Spanish folk legend and libertine Don Juan as an unsophisticated, innocent young man who delighted in being seduced by the beautiful women who pursued him. Donna Julia was the first in a long line of women who seduced Don Juan, (or were seduced by him).

Sent abroad by his mother, he survived a shipwreck and was cast up on a Greek island.

Fig 34
Don Juan et Haidee
Dans La Grotte

Sold into slavery in Constantinople, he escaped and joined the Russian army and was sent to St Petersburg, where he won the favour of Catherine the Great. She sent him on a diplomatic mission to England.

John Murray entreated Byron to use his *"most tasteful discretion and leave out certain prominations to indelicacy."*

Byron was prepared to make only minor changes:

"With regard to the Poeshie, I will have no 'cutting and slashing'... Don Juan shall be an entire horse, or none." (Byron - Letter to Hobhouse)

Don Juan reflected a very different style of hero to *Childe Harold* and revealed other sides of Byron's character and personality. A romance and epic adventure, it proved controversial because it laughed at religion, attacked public figures and made fun of society's values. Upon their publication in 1819, cantos 1 and 2 were widely criticised.

The Blackwood's Edinburgh Magazine denounced *Don Juan* as a

"filthy and impious poem." Byron was clearly not in agreement:
"Don Juan will be known by and bye for what it is intended - a satire on abuses of the present states of society - It may be now and then voluptuous - I can't help that... No girl will ever be seduced by reading Don Juan." (Byron)

At the time of his death in 1824, Byron had completed 16 out of 17 cantos; canto 17 remained unfinished. Clearly while some readers found *Don Juan "a filthy and impious poem,"* others considered it *"his finest and most entertaining"* poetry. A famous quote from *Don Juan*, used to this day is - *'For truth is always strange; Stranger than fiction.'*

The Vision of Judgement 1822

The Poet Laureate Robert Southey had published an adulatory poem in memory of George III - *A Vision of Judgement*. In the preface he attacked certain unnamed poets and called them 'satanic' in reference to their "Satanic spirit of pride and audacious impiety."

Byron responded in 1822 with **The** *Vision of Judgement* - a satire on Southey's poem and King George III. Hunt published *The Vision of Judgement* in The Liberal - a short-lived periodical founded in 1822 by Shelley, Byron and Leigh Hunt.

The Deformed Transformed 1822

An unfinished drama which told the story of Arnold – a deformed hunchback, rejected by his mother. Arnold planned on killing himself but was prevented by the miraculous apparition of the 'Stranger' offering to exchange his crippled body for that of a male beauty in the hero of his choosing. Arnold opted for Achilles.

Sardanapalus 1821

A lesser known play which Byron dedicated to Goethe. It went on to inspire musical work by Liszt, Berlioz and Ravel and the famous painting by Eugene Delacroix.
Sardanapalus was a decadent Assyrian ruler in ancient times. In response to a major military defeat, he ordered the death of his horses, slaves and concubines. He then made a huge pyre upon which he burned himself to death.

There are some very impactful short pieces which reflect particular events in the life of Lord Byron.

Byron's Oak 1807

George Byron planted the seedling in 1798, on his first visit to Newstead Abbey at the age of ten. He returned after University at the age of nineteen, and expressed his disappointment at its lack of progress and the fact that it was choked with weeds.

Fig 35
Byron's Oak
c.1900

"Young Oak! when I planted thee deep in the ground,
I hoped that your days would be longer than mine
That thy dark waving branches would flourish around
And ivy thy trunk with its mantle entwine."

The Dream 1816

The poem described Annesley Park and Hall and examples of Byron's adolescent passion for his neighbour Mary Anne Chaworth. It recorded their meetings on Diadem Hill and their final parting at Annesley Hall.

"I've seen my bride another's bride-
Have seen her seated by his side,-
Have seen the infant which she bore
Wear the sweet smile her mother bore

When she and I in youth have smiled
As fond and faultless as her child.
Have seen her eyes, in cold disdain,
Ask if I felt no secret pain.''

She Walks in Beauty (Hebrew Melodies 1814)

The short lyrical poem of praise was inspired by Byron's first sight of his cousin by marriage, Anne Beatrix Wilmot. Recently widowed, she attended a party in a deep black mourning dress with glittering spangles. The poem was written overnight.

''She walks in beauty, like the night
Of cloudless climes and starry skies;
And all that's best of dark and bright
Meet in her aspect and her eyes;
Thus mellowed to that tender light
Which heaven to gaudy day denies.''

11c. Poet's Chronological Timeline

England 1806 - 1809
Fugitive Pieces – printed and withdrawn
Poems on Various Occasions
Hours of Idleness – 1st edition sold out in 6 months
Poems Original and Translated
English Bards and Scotch Reviewers

Mediterranean Travels: 1809 - 1811
Hints of Horace – written at the Capuchin Monastery in Athens
The Curse of Minerva – a scornful response to the removal of the Elgin Marbles
Childe Harold's Pilgrimage – start of cantos 1&2

England 1812 - 1816

Childe Harold's Pilgrimage – the First Edition of cantos 1&2 sold out in 3 days

The Giaour – First Turkish Tale

The Bride of Abydos

The Corsair – sold 10,000 copies on the first day of its publication

Ode to Napoleon Bonaparte

Lara - final Turkish Tale

A selection of Hebrew Melodies – Byron's poetry put to music by Isaac Nathan

1816: The Siege of Corinth

1816: Parisina

1816: Fare Thee Well – an autobiographical poem which bade farewell to his wife and daughter

1816: A Sketch from Private Life – a second poem about the separation

Self-imposed Exile 1816-1824

Switzerland 1816

1816: The Dream – captured his boyhood passion for Mary Chaworth

1816: Darkness – a dream about an apocalyptic end of the world

1816-1817: Manfred

1816-1817: The Prisoner of Chillon

Italy: Venice and Rome 1816 - 1819

Childe Harold's Pilgrimage – canto 3 published

Beppo – a light-hearted Venetian story; published anonymously

Don Juan – cantos 1,2 &3

Childe Harold's Pilgrimage – canto 4

Mazzeppa

Italy: Ravenna 1819 - 1821
Don Juan – canto 4
Don Juan – canto 5
Marino Faliero Doge of Venice
The Two Foscari
Cain
Sardanapalus
The Vision of Judgement
The Blues
Heaven and Earth

Italy: Pisa Venice and Genoa 1822 - 1823
Don Juan – cantos 6-9
Werner – a tragedy and play
The Age of Bronze
The Island – Christian and his Comrades – based upon the Mutiny
on the Bounty in the South Seas
Deformed Transformed
Don Juan – cantos 10-12 and cantos 13–16

Greece: Missolonghi 1824
Love and Death
On January 22nd 1824, Byron composed his last final poem to mark
his 36th birthday. A private diary entry, it reflected his participation
in the Greek War of Independence. It included a declaration of his
unrequited love for Lukas Chalandritsanos, his Greek page:

> *''Thus much and more; and yet thou lov'st me not,*
> *And never wilt! Love dwells not in our will.*
> *Nor can I blame thee, though it be my lot*
> *To strongly, wrongly, vainly love thee still.''*

12. THE YEARS OF SELF-IMPOSED EXILE

On April 25th 1816, Byron left England with his Napoleonic travelling coach, accompanied by Robert Rushton and William Fletcher plus Dr John William Polidori (personal physician); Scrope Davies and John Cam Hobhouse. The exposure of past sexual relationships, the failure of his marriage and his crushing debts were key motivators behind the departure from his homeland. Suspicions of incest with his half-sister had circulated more widely and Byron wished to protect her from scandal.

''My dearest love, I have never ceased nor can cease to feel for a moment that perfect and bondless attachment which binds me to you, which renders me utterly incapable of real love for any other human being. A thousand loves to you from me – which is very generous, for I only ask one in return. – Ever dearest Byron.''
(Farewell to Augusta Leigh)

SWITZERLAND 1816

Lake Geneva
The party crossed the sea from Dover to Ostend. They stopped first in the Netherlands, and then travelled along the Rhine to Geneva in the Swiss Alps. In Secheron, Byron stayed at Hotel Angleterre and met up with Percy Bysshe Shelley. Shelley had been sent down from Oxford University after he published a pamphlet entitled 'The necessity of atheism'. He was accompanied by Mary Wollstonecraft Godwin and Mary's stepsister, Claire Godwin Clairmont. Shelley's belief in Byron helped to restore his shattered confidence. Having had a brief affair with Byron in London, Claire Clairmont had high expectations of renewing the relationship.

Byron stayed at Villa Diodati on Lake Geneva where the party composed their famous ghost stories. Mary was the outright winner of the competition with her Gothic novel - Frankenstein; or, The Modern Prometheus. John William Polidori, having listened to Byron on the subject of the Greek superstition about vampires, moved the setting of The Vampyre from the likes of Bulgaria (Eastern Europe) to England and Greece.

The Shelleys returned to England with Claire Clairmont, pregnant with Byron's child. Clara Allegra Byron was born in Bath on January 12th 1817. John Cam Hobhouse and Scrope Davies arrived in Geneva and, along with Polidori, they all visited Chamonix and Mont Blanc. At this point Robert Rushton was returned to England and Polidori dismissed. Byron and Hobhouse headed for Italy.

ITALY 1816- 1821

Venice 1816-1819

Initially Byron was focused upon his poetry and his writings were influenced by his surroundings. He was enamoured with Italy and Venetian history. The Bridge of Sighs was so called by Lord Byron.

''I stood in Venice on the bridge of Sighs,
 A palace and a prison on either hand ''

Byron enjoyed horse riding and frequently swam between Venice and the island of Lido. He became a bit of a philanderer - his longest affairs were with Marianna Segati, landlord and draper's wife, and Margarita Cogni, a baker's wife. He learnt Albanian with Father Harutyun at the Monastery of Mekhitarists and the abbots at the Monastery on the island of San Lazzaro. He became immersed in Armenian culture and language and helped to compile an English Armenian dictionary.

1817: Byron visited Ferrara, Florence and Rome. He returned to Venice in 1818 and initially rented a Casino (little house). It was here that he wrote the 4th canto of *Childe Harold* based on his journey to Rome. Having sold Newstead Abbey, Byron rented a new residence – the Palazzo Mocenigo on the Grand Canal. He arrived there with his servants, William Fletcher and Tita (the gondolier Giovanni Battista Falcieri) plus his menagerie of animals:

"Lord B's establishment consists, besides servants, of ten horses, eight enormous dogs, three monkeys, five cats, an eagle,a crow,and a falcon; and all these, except the horses,walk about the house,which every now and then resounds with their unarbitrated quarrels, as if they were the masters of it."

"I find that my enumeration of the animals in this Circean Palace was defective... I have just met on the grand staircase five peacocks, two guinea hens, and an Egyptian crane." (Percy Bysshe Shelley)

Here Byron wrote the comic poem *Beppo* and the 1st canto of *Don Juan*. It was a period of womanising and/or sexual bragging - *'several women in a single day'* and *'200'* liaisons in less than three years.

1818: Shelley arrived in Italy now married to Mary (after the suicide of his first wife Harriet). They were accompanied by Claire Clairmont who arrived with Allegra (one year old) and a nurse. Allegra was sent to Venice with her nurse to spend time with her father. A proud father, Byron loved and spoiled his baby girl.

1819: Byron met the Contessa Teresa Guiccioli (aged nineteen) - *"My only and last love."* She was a high spirited, intelligent and attractive lady of great charm and demure self-confidence. Teresa was the 3rd wife of Count Alessandro Guiccioli - an Italian nobleman (in his late fifties).

Her father Count Ruggero Gamba was a committed republican seeking freedom for Italy from rule by the Pope and the Austrians.

Ravenna 1819-1821

Byron wanted to be close to his beloved Teresa, and moved to Ravenna in 1819. He rented the apartments on the first floor of the Palazzo Guiccioli and was accepted as the Contessa's official lover.

He brought all his furniture, servants and animals with him and became her Cicisbeo - Cavalier Servente.
"I am in love and tired of promiscuous concubinage and have the opportunity of settling for life." (Byron)

Count Guiccioli was one of the most powerful men in Italy. He was concerned about the intimacy of their relationship. Whilst back in Venice, he arrived unexpectedly with the intention of taking Teresa home. He presented his wife with a list of demands regarding her future conduct. There had been some concern that Byron and Teresa might elope together.
In 1820, Byron visited the Shelleys in Pisa. This was where Byron first met Alexandros Mavrokordatos. Shelley considered him to be the most intellectually gifted amongst the political leaders of Greece - highly educated and a nationalist with liberal leanings. He assisted Mary with her Greek and in return she taught him English.
"She has been a Greek student several months and is reading Antigone with our turbaned friend who in return is taught English."(Percy Bysshe Shelley)

In Ravenna, Byron was warmly welcomed by the Gamba family, all of whom were aristocratic republicans. Byron met Pietro Gamba, Teresa's brother, for the first time on his return from studying in Rome (aged twenty). Pietro clearly exhibited the same enthusiasm for revolutionary politics, and encouraged Byron to join the secret society of Carbonari (charcoal burners), who sought freedom from oppression and the unification of Italy.
Teresa was granted a legal separation from Count Guiccioli. The terms dictated that she lived either with her father or in a convent. Byron was given control over the group of Ravenna Carbonari as armsman of the Cacciatori Americani (American Hunters). He bought guns, bayonets and bullets to arm the troops.

"There is something so exciting in the idea of the greatest poet of the day sacrificing his fortune, his occupations, his enjoyments - in short offering up on the altar of Liberty all the immense advantages which station, fortune and genius can bestow." (Lady Blessington - Irish novelist and journalist)

By 1821, Byron had become disillusioned and disappointed by the behaviour of members of the Carbonari. He felt he was being used. *"My lower apartments are full of their bayonets, fusils, cartridges and what not. I suppose they consider me a depot, to be sacrificed, in case of accidents."* (Byron)

An uprising was planned but suspended by the appearance of the Papal States Army (Austrians) on the River Po. The Carbonari movement in Northern Italy collapsed. After the revolt failed, Pietro Gamba was arrested and sent into exile, along with his father Count Ruggero.

Byron had arranged for Allegra to be educated at the girls' boarding school run by the nuns in a convent at Bagnocavallo, near Ravenna. She died of a fever the following year at the age of five. She received no visits from her father prior to her death, despite her letter to him written in Italian (no doubt assisted by nuns), in September 1821.

Byron asked John Murray for his assistance in organising her burial back in England at Harrow Church. He recalled the spot in the Churchyard where he used to sit for hours on end and wished Allegra to be buried inside the church - near to the entrance.
"It is my present intention to send her remains to England for sepulture in Harrow Church (where I once hoped to have laid my own) - I wish the funeral to be very private." (Byron - Letter to John Murray)

He wrote an inscription for her gravestone, concluding:
"I shall go to her, but she shall not return to me."

Because of her illegitimacy, Allegra was in fact, buried at the entrance to the church without a marker.

The churchyard of Harrow on the Hill held happy memories of childhood for Byron.
"A tomb under a large tree (bearing the name of Peachie, or Peachey), where I used to sit for hours and hours as a boy. This was my favourite spot." (Byron - Letter to John Murray)

Lord Byron sat dreaming by the 'Peachy Tomb' in St Mary's graveyard.

Fig 36
Engraving by Edward Finden

Pisa 1821 - 1822

1821: Byron returned to Casa Lanfranchi while Teresa, in accordance with the terms of her separation, resided with her father and her brother a few short streets away. The Pisan Circle was formed - George Byron, John Taaffe, Edward John Trelawny, Edward Williams and wife Jane, plus the Shelleys and Thomas Medwin (Shelley's cousin).

Leigh Hunt had co-founded, along with his brother, 'The Examiner' in England. It had proved to be a leading intellectual journal supporting radical principles. Shelley invited Hunt, on Byron's behalf, to be the joint editor of a new literary journal - 'The Liberal.'

"He (Byron) proposes that you should come out and go shares with him and me in a periodical work, to be conducted here; in which each of the contracting parties shall publish all their original compositions, and share the profits." (Letter from Percy Shelley to Leigh Hunt)

1822: Byron, in the company of Pietro Gamba, Taaffe, Captain Hay, Trelawny and Shelley were returning from their ride when a member of the local garrison on horseback, Sergeant-Major Stefani Massi, dashed at full speed through the midst of the party, violently jostling one of them. They pursued Massi to the city gate where, following an altercation, Massi sought to have them arrested. Subsequently, Massi was stabbed with a pitchfork by one of the servants. He was severely hurt, but not mortally wounded. Following the Massi affair, Byron and the Shelleys left Pisa.

Montenegro 1822

Byron signed a six month lease on Villa Dupuy, located in the hills close to Livorno. His schooner, the Bolivar, arrived carrying cannons. On July 1st, Percy Bysshe Shelley and Captain Edward Williams sailed the Don Juan to Livorno, in the Tuscany region of Italy. Shelley met up with Leigh Hunt and Byron to discuss the new journal - 'The Liberal'. After the meeting, on July 8th, Shelley, Williams and the boat boy sailed out of Livorno and headed for Lerici, situated on the coast of the Gulf of La Spezia.

The boat went down in a sudden storm on the Bay of Spezia and both men were drowned. They were washed ashore some ten days later *'disfigured and in a state of putrefaction'*. The bodies were initially buried in the sand. They then had to be dug up, and burned on a pyre on the beach a month later. Shelley's ashes were buried in Rome. The heart was eventually buried back in England.

Fig 37
*Imaginary
recreation of the
cremation
by Louis Fournier*
.

Following the cremation, Byron swam to and from the Bolivar, a distance of some three miles, in the heat of the midday sun. There were serious consequences - a feverish attack, skin peeling off and severe pain.

Byron's tribute to Shelley amounted to war -
"His thoughts reared round to his early love, the Isles of Greece, and the revolution in that country for before that time he never dreamt of donning the warrior's plume though the peace-loving Shelley had suggested and I urged it." (Edward Trelawny)

His relationship with Teresa and concerns regarding her safety were a constant worry and may have delayed any immediate plans Byron may have had at this stage. However, while Byron probably never stopped loving Teresa as such, there were signs that he was becoming restless and that his commitment to the relationship was being eroded by day-to-day living.
"He is kept in excellent order, quarrelled with and hen-pecked to his heart's content." (Mary Shelley communicating with Jane Williams)
"Lord Byron is fixed on Greece - he gets rid of two burdens - the Gucciolies and The Liberal." (Mary Shelley)

13. THE RISE OF NATIONALISM IN EUROPE

Background

The French Revolution, by destroying the traditional structures of power, was instrumental in political transformation. National awakening also grew out of an intellectual reaction to the Enlightenment - a philosophical movement that advocated liberty, constitutional government and separation of church and state.

Success came first in Greece where an eight year war against Ottoman rule led to an Independent Greek State. At the battle of Navarino, combined British, French and Russian forces annihilated the Ottoman fleet paving the way for Greek Independence.

The Grand Tour provided young men and women from the British upper class with the opportunity to discover the cultural wonders of Europe and understand the history of Western civilisation.

It became a regular feature of aristocratic education. Byron's own travels had stimulated a love and passion for Greece, its people and its culture. His own style of Graecomania.

Philhellenism was an intellectual movement of both non-Greeks who were passionate about ancient Greek culture, and Greeks who patriotically supported their own country and culture. The title is derived from the words Philos (friend/lover) and Hellen (a Greek). The Greek Philhellenes who had either emigrated to other parts of Europe, or had been born there, were more aware of the American War of Independence and/or the Napoleonic Wars and the subsequent chaos and violence that they caused. They were also influenced by the Age of Enlightenment which supported modernisation, individual liberty and religious tolerance, whilst opposing an absolute monarchy and the power of religious authorities.

Typically Philhellenes were classical scholars, idealists, poets and radical politicians who looked to provide moral, material and military support. The 19th century German Druden dictionary definition was:
'A political-romantic movement, which supported the liberation struggle of the Greeks against the Turks.'

Byron perceived a moral obligation for Europe to restore liberty to Greece as payment for the civilisation which Greece had given to the world. His own political concepts were related to political liberalism and a constitutional Greek government. He was more realistic than the typical Philhellene regarding the nature and character of the Greeks themselves. In this context Byron may be described as 'a new age Philhellene'. Percy Bysshe Shelley was the more archetypal supporter, fully committed to the Philhellenic 'dream'.

"We are all Greeks. Our laws, our literature, our religion, our art have their roots in Greece. But for Greece, we might still have been savages and idolaters... The modern Greek is the descendant of those glorious beings whom the imagination almost refuses to figure to itself as belonging to our kind, and he inherits much of their sensibility, their rapidity of conception, and their courage."
(Preface to Shelley's poem Hellas - dedicated to Prince Alexander Mavrocordatos)

War broke out in 1821 when Lord Byron was in Italy. Support for The Cause varied in intensity and participation across Europe. Some volunteered to go and fight in Greece while others were actively operating in their own country to lend moral and material assistance.

Byron in Genoa 1823
Byron had moved to Casa Saluzzo (palace) along with Teresa and Pietro Gamba. It was whilst in Genoa, that Byron started to think seriously about supporting the Greek War of Independence.
"In short - the longer I live - the more I perceive that money (honestly come by) is the Philosopher's stone... I want to get a sum together to go amongst the Greeks ... and do some good." (Byron)

Having identified the opportunity to provide assistance for the war in Greece, Byron's interests moved away from poetry.
"With his usual love for mystification he had decided in his own mind to join their cause. In Byron there were, as I have said, two natures – the man and the poet were different entities."(Thomas Medwin - writer and poet)

In March 1823, the London Greek Committee was formed by John Bowering and Edward Blaquiere. Its aim was to support the Greek War by raising funds by subscription for military supplies and loans to stabilise a fledgling Greek government.

The Committee decided to send Edward Blaquiere to Greece to report on what was happening there and to visit Byron in Genoa to encourage him to join the Committee. Lord Byron and John Cam Hobhouse were amongst its first members. Byron promised to help in any way he could and expressed his willingness to go himself to Greece. He wrote *The Isles of Greece* in support of the Greek War.

> *"The mountains look on Marathon*
> *And Marathon looks on the sea -*
> *And musing there an hour alone,*
> *I dream'd that Greece might yet be free*
> *For, standing on the Persians' grave*
> *I could not deem myself a slave."*

Still stranded in Genoa, Lord Byron had a lot of pertinent issues to consider:
- His 'circle of friends' in Pisa had broken up after Shelley's death
- He was disillusioned with the Carbonari and somewhat bored of his life in Genoa
- His genuine passion for Teresa had faded somewhat and it would not be safe to take her to a war zone
- He was ageing prematurely
- There was a need to reinvent himself and find a new source of adventure - and fame

"Opposition and the prospect of the greatest dangers were to him the most alluring excitements." (Pietro Gamba's Journal)

Then everything started to fall into place-
- Going to Greece on behalf of the London Greek Committee would be an exciting new adventure - he might even be able to go into battle and fight
- Teresa was prepared (albeit reluctantly) to return to the safety of her father's home in Ravenna
- He was in a unique position to help based on his aristocratic status and fame - as well as his wealth
- The Greek Cause would be a worthy use of his inheritance

"With a certain sum in advance and no particular occupation, how could I better employ my time and money" (Byron)

Byron estimated that he had £20,000 (approaching £2.5 million) at his disposal - all of which he planned to spend. He wrote to the Committee and expressed his desire to visit Greece in person. He then wrote to Edward Trelawny and asked him to accompany him. *"I can do nothing without you, and am exceeding anxious to see you... They all say I can be of use to Greece; I do not know how - nor do they; but at all events, let us go." (Byron - Letter to Edward Trelawny)*

Byron felt the need to put the capital he had received from the sale of property in England to good use. To this end he sold the Bolivar, his 'pleasure boat,' and chartered an English brig - Hercules. He purchased scarlet and gold military uniforms, swords and firearms, and three helmets for Pietro Gamba, Edward Trelawny and himself. Made to Byron's own specification, the helmet and sword were inspired by the description of Hector's armour in the Iliad.

Byron waited for letters of confirmation and instructions until mid-July. When none arrived, he went aboard the Hercules, accompanied by Edward Trelawny, Pietro Gamba, Lega Zambelli (secretary) and Francesco Bruno (young Italian doctor) - along with five horses. They were accompanied by eight servants including Tita Falcieri (ex-gondolier), William Fletcher (valet) and Benjamin Lewis (Trelawny's black American servant). Count Skilitzy (a Greek on his way back from Russia) was granted passage. The ship carried 10,000 in Spanish dollars and bills of exchange for 40,000 more. In addition, there were chests of medical stores, arms and ammunition to be conveyed to Greece.

They departed on July 14th. In the night strong westerly winds arose which damaged the Hercules and they were forced to return to Genoa. Once the damage was repaired, the Hercules set sail for Leghorn (the Italian port city of Livorno) and on to the Ionian Islands. Byron's spirits were high. He slept on the open deck and enjoyed the sports that he had loved in his youth - pistol shooting, fencing and boxing.

The Hercules anchored at Argostoli, the main port, capital and administrative centre of Cephalonia. Upon their arrival, it was evident that Blaquiere had already returned to England, to report to the Greek Committee. Furthermore, there were no letters from Archbishop Ignazio of Arta with introductions to the principal Greek chiefs and the government. Byron's mission had effectively been placed on hold.

14. THE GREEK WAR OF INDEPENDENCE

For three and a half centuries, Greece had been ruled by Turks. It was a part of the Ottoman Empire under the Sultan of Constantinople. The Greek revolutionary secret society - the Philiki Etaireia (Friendly Brotherhood) was formed by merchants in Odessa (Ukraine) in 1814. They were mostly Phanariot Greeks from Russia, local chieftains from Greece and Serbs. They played a vital role in the initial uprising which led to the Greek War of Independence. Their motto proved to be one of the most famous sayings of the revolution - 'Freedom or Death.'

14a. The Early Stages of the Greek War 1821-1823

1821
Alexandros Ypsilantis, a prince and high-ranking officer in the Imperial Russian cavalry, had been made Leader of the Philiki Etaireia in 1820. He declared a revolt against the Ottoman Empire, and raised the first flag on February 24th in Moldavia.
Bishop Germanos of Patras proclaimed the Greek national uprising and raised the revolutionary flag outside the Monastery of Agia Lavra on March 25th.
The fall of the fortress of Monemvasia was an early success for the Greek forces. The fortress was besieged by land and sea and after four months it was surrendered to the Greeks. Navarino and Tripolitsa were next to fall.
The Battle of Alamana in April, was a military defeat for the Greeks. The heroic martyrdom of the Greek leader Athanasios Diakos raised awareness and sympathy for the Greek Cause.
The Battle of Dragasani in Wallachia saw the destruction of the forces of the Philiki Etaireia by the forces of Sultan Mahmud II. It ended the first insurrection of the Greek War of Independence.

1822

The Greek Constitution of 1822 was adopted by the First National Assembly at Epidaurus. It attempted to achieve a temporary Hellenic government and military organisation until a National Government could be formed. Alexandros Mavrokordatos took office as President of the Executive.

The massacre on the island of Chios by Ottoman troops in March resulted in the deaths of tens of thousands of Greeks. The Ottoman forces slaughtered, looted, took prisoners and decimated the island's population. This massacre of christians provoked international outrage and led to increased support for the Greek Cause.

The battle of Peta in Arta, was fought by Alexandros Mavrokordatos and Markos Botsaris against Ottoman forces led by Omer Vrioni. The betrayal of Georgios Bakolas contributed to the defeat of Greek forces. The defeat seriously impacted upon Mavrokordatos' status as a leader.

The first siege of Missolonghi saw the Ottoman forces attempt to capture the port town. Missolonghi had gained importance during the course of the war due to its strategic position. At the start of the war, the Greeks had taken possession of the city and fortified it. In 1822 it was besieged by Ottoman forces without success.

The battle of Nauplia saw a series of naval engagements between the Greek and Ottoman fleets. Frank Abney Hastings distinguished himself while in charge of the island fort. This experience convinced him of the need to reform the fleet to make it a more effective force against the Turks. Frank Abney Hastings was a British naval officer and Philhellene. He had served in the Royal Navy and travelled to Greece to aid the Greeks.

The destruction of the Ottoman Army at Dervenakia in August proved to be a decisive Greek victory. The destruction of Dramali Pasha's forces saved the Morea - the heartland of the rebellion.

During this time, many Europeans arrived in Greece to fight. Others were involved in war operations and raising funds. Philhellenic Societies sprang up first in Germany, France and Switzerland.

1823
During 1822, the Greeks had been relatively successful in their war against the Turks. However, with no Turks to fight, they turned on each other.
"Each faction had its agents, exerting every art to degrade its opponent."(Pietro Gamba's Journal)

Byron had not been optimistic regarding his own ability to assist in the Greek War of Independence. There were issues concerning his own capabilities and state of health, as well as his observations regarding the social, political and economic differences and divisions amongst the various Greek factions.
"The one I am about to undertake is not the least, though probably, it will be the last; for, with my broken health, and the chances of war, Greece will most likely terminate my mortal career." (Byron)
"To engage in a cause, for the successful result of which I have no very sanguine hopes."(Byron)

Weeks passed and Byron had not heard from either John Cam Hobhouse or the Committee. However, Metropolitan Ignatius, spiritual leader and mentor of Mavrokordatos, seemed to be aware that Lord Byron was already on his way to Greece.
"The nobleman Lord Byron is on his way to see the state of affairs in Greece and to lend a helping hand. He has means. He is a member of the committee established in London in favour of the Greeks; he has important friends and can bring benefit, provided he is pleased and our compatriots can win him over with their good offices towards him." (Metropolitan Ignatius, spiritual leader and mentor of Mavrokordatos)

The Greece Byron was about to encounter differed significantly from the Greece he had seen during his Mediterranean travels. As a result of the wars which had already taken place, Greece now had four independent territories:

1. The Peloponnese - controlled by Theodoros Kolokotronis and lesser warlords.
2. West of the Mainland - where Alexandros Mavrokordatos was regarded as a leader, based in the capital Missolonghi.
3. Central Greece - where commander-in-chief, Odysseas Androutsos, ruled undisputedly from the Acropolis of Athens.
4. The Greek Islands - with no obvious leader, but a significant number of ship-owners and sea captains who had transformed the Merchant Navy and were in control of naval routes.

Struggles amongst the Greek leaders and their followers resulted in deep-seated divisions.
"The Greeks were more intent on persecuting and calumniating each other than on securing the independence of their country... There was more to be feared from their own dissensions than from the Turks." (Pietro Gamba Journal 1835)

As far as Byron's objectives were concerned, there were essentially two key combatants:
Theodoros Kolokotronis - Chief warlord and strongly influenced by the revolutionary ideas of the Napoleonic era. On the outbreak of war, he formed a confederation of Moreot klept bands (warriors/brigands). Considered a 'genius' at guerrilla warfare, he is well remembered as the klept hero and commander-in-chief of the Peloponnese. He is often considered to be the preeminent leader of the Greek War of Independence.

His armaments were largely British as a result of his service in the Greek volunteer regiment of the British army in Zakynthos and his time as a Major during the Napoleonic Wars.

Fig 38
*Theodoros Kolokotronis
by Dionysios Tsokos*

Prince Alexandros Mavrokordatos - Chief Moderniser. A wealthy, well-educated Phanariot Greek, he envisaged a modern Greek state with a Western European orientation. He was thus popular with the European Philhellenes. A constitutional nationalist and liberal politician, he was focused upon a strong central government. Alexandros Mavrokordatos was celebrated for writing Greece's Declaration of Independence. He was elected President of The First National Assembly in January 1822.

Byron had previously met Mavrokordatos in Pisa, at the Shelleys residence, in 1820.

Fig 39
*Prince Alexandros Mavrokordatos
by Adam Friedel*

To this day he is considered something of an enigmatic leader. While some felt he had a kindly disposition and was cleverer than other leaders, others felt he was cunning and devious. Either way, he was sincere in wanting a constitutional republic and his relationship with Byron was of fundamental importance to the regeneration of a nation.

One wonders if Byron ever met **Princess Manto Mavrogenous**. They certainly met in the Greek film in 1971. But if they had, then surely we would know more about it. She had studied ancient Greek philosophy and history and spoke French, Italian and Turkish fluently. When the war began she went to Mykonos and encouraged the leaders to join the revolution.

An extremely wealthy aristocrat, she contributed her fortune to the Hellenic Cause. She had grown up in an educated family, influenced by the Age of Enlightenment.

Fig 40
Princess Manto Mavrogenous
by Adam Friedel

She equipped and manned her own ships. For the battle in Karystos in 1822, she had put together a fleet of six ships and infantry. She financed and equipped men to fight in the first siege of Missolonghi. She moved to Nafplio in 1823 to be in the centre of the struggle.

Under her encouragement, her aristocratic European friends contributed both money and arms. When the war was over, Ioannis Kapodistrias (Governor of Greece), awarded her the rank of Lieutenant General and granted her a dwelling in Nafplio. Mavrogenous was depicted on the reverse of the Greek 2-drachma coin in 1988-2001.

Byron still awaiting instructions in Cephalonia

In August 1823, Byron had sailed to Cephalonia where he waited nearly four months for instructions from The Greek Committee in London.
"As the Committee has not favoured me with any specific instructions... I of course have to suppose that I am left to my own discretion." (Byron)

Around this time, Mavrocordatos had been threatened by warlords. He abandoned the Morea, quit public affairs and sought refuge in Hydra.
In August, Byron spent eight days in Ithaca (home of Ulysses). It was here that Byron's benevolent feelings toward the victims of war were displayed. Families had fled from Chios, Patras and other parts of Greece. Byron gave the commandant 3,000 piastres for their relief, and persuaded a destitute family to return with him to Cephalonia.
"Induced a family, once rich in Patras, but now reduced to the greatest misery, to pass over to Cephalonia, where he provided them with a house, and assigned them a monthly allowance."(Pietro Gamba's Journal)

This was where and how Byron met Loukas Chalandritsanos (c.fifteen years of age) whom he employed as his page until his death in 1824.

In his Journal, Gamba claimed that despite the hot weather, Byron enjoyed good health and spirits:

"We had been eight days absent travelling generally from nine in the morning until four or five in the evening… under a most scorching sun. Lord Byron never enjoyed better health or spirits." (Pietro Gamba's Journal)

However, toward the end of the holiday, Byron could not be dissuaded from swimming for long periods of time, in the heat of the midday sun. Later in the day, the party visited a convent where priests were stunned by Byron's apoplectic rage.

"He gradually lashed himself into one of those ungovernable torrents of rage, to which at times he was liable; the paroxysm increased so as almost to divest him of reason, and I really entertained apprehensions of an apoplectic attack… Snatching a lamp like one possessed, he cried out "my head is burning; will no one relieve me from the presence of this pestilential madman?"(James Hamilton Browne - Narrative of a Visit, in 1823, to the Seat of War in Greece)

In October – Pasha Omer Vrioni of Ioannina and Mustai of Skodra (leading Ottomans) approached Missolonghi with a sizable army of Albanian Muslims loyal to the Sultan. With the support of a naval blockade of vessels, they laid siege to the town.

"Missolonghi is blockaded by sea and besieged by land; the town is short of provisions and sure to fall to the Turks."(Mavrokordatos)

Frank Abney Hastings had already written to Byron and explained that Greece could not win the war without superiority at sea. Emissaries had been sent to London to ask for funds to activate the fleet. In the meantime, on the sale of the Rochdale estate, Byron agreed a loan of £4,000 to pay sailors and reactivate the Greek fleet. They sailed from Hydra and Spetses and arrived in Missolonghi in early December. In response, the Turks withdrew both naval and land forces.

Byron took charge of 40 Souliotes to be his body-guard. The Souliotes were an Orthodox Christian Albanian tribal community from the mountainous region of North West Greece.
"They were distinguished amongst the warriors of Roumelia for their courage and experience, and, above all, for their fidelity."(Pietro Gamba's Journal)

Byron was appointed 'principal agent of the Greek Committee.' He was instructed only to express his intentions of devoting his fortune to their cause (not placing himself at their disposal or committing to anything).
"I believed myself on a fool's errand from the outset... I will at least linger on here or there till I see whether I can be of any service in any way."(Byron - Letter to Charles James Napier, Governor of Cephalonia)

Byron was besieged by representatives of the different factions and was well aware of the their objectives - and the Grecian style of approach:
"You will be received here as a saviour. Be assured, My Lord, that it depends only on yourself to secure the destiny of Greece."(Letter from Mavrokordatos to Byron)
"These Greeks are excellent flatterers. I do not believe they care one farthing about me personally though they would be glad to get my money."(Conversation with James Kennedy)

Byron's intentions could not have been more transparent:
"I can recognise only the Greek Government - without reference to the persons who compose it… As a foreigner I have nothing to do with factions or private preferences of individuals." (Byron)

Having spent his own money fighting for the Cause, Mavrocordatos identified Lord Byron as a way of achieving his aims and wrote to him directly. Byron was already well disposed toward Mavrokordatos, having met him before. Charles James Napier, the governor of Cephalonia, also thought highly of him.

Pietro Gamba had expressed the opinion that Byron would continue to wait until he was able to identify the right moment and the right beneficiary. Was this the moment that Byron finally decided to support Alexandros Mavrokordatos as Commander-in-chief and Governor of Western Greece. Cephalonia had indeed seen Byron's final transformation into an embryonic statesman and political leader, fully committed to the Cause.

In November, Colonel L Stanhope arrived and Byron was declared the representative of both the English and German Committees. He wrote letters regarding the Civil War:

"Unless union and order are established all hopes of a loan will be vain; and all the assistance which the Greeks could expect from abroad - assistance neither trifling nor worthless - will be suspended or destroyed."(Pietro Gamba's Journal)

In December he wrote emphatically to Mavrokordatos, that Greece must now choose one of three possible courses - and act swiftly:

"Greece is, at present, placed between three measures: either to re-conquer her liberty, to become a dependence of the sovereigns of Europe, or to return to a Turkish province. Civil War is but a road which leads to the other two later." (Pietro Gamba's Journal)

Around the time Mavrocordatos arrived in Missolonghi as Governor-General of the province, Byron had received a letter from the Legislative body asking him to cooperate with Mavrocordatos. Byron agreed to take Souliotes into his pay and to lead them in an attack upon the fortress of Lepanto.

Lord Byron boarded the light, fast-sailing Mistico with Bruno, Fletcher and Loukas. A larger vessel, the Bombarda, with Pietro Gamba in charge, conveyed the servants, baggage, horses, armaments etc. They sailed to Zante to pick up 'a considerable amount of money.'

Crossing over to Missolonghi, Byron's vessel came close to a Turkish frigate and was forced to take refuge at Dragomestri.

The Bombarda was captured by the frigate. Luck would have it that the captain recognised Count Gamba as the man who had previously saved his life, as well as that of his brother and other sailors. He persuaded Yusuf Pasha (Commander at Patras) to release the vessel and free those aboard. The fact that Yusuf Pasha had no right to detain a vessel carrying a neutral flag and under British protection, had been blatantly ignored.

On the evening of January 4th 1824, Byron sailed through the Gulf of Patras and into the lagoon at Missolonghi.

14b. The Hero Of Missolonghi 1824

At 11.00am on January 5th, Lord Byron went ashore at Missolonghi, amidst the mosquito-infested marshes which spread malaria infections. He was dressed in his scarlet regimental uniform.

Imaginary painting of Byron's reception at Missolonghi - Dressed as an aristocratic poet and not in regimental uniform.

Fig 41
by Theodoros Vryzakakis (1861)

His arrival was welcomed with salvos of artillery, musket fire and wild music. Crowds of soldiers and citizens had assembled on the shore. He was awarded freedom of the city and shown to the house where he would reside with Col. Leicester Stanhope.

Stanhope is best known for his introduction of the printing press into Greece and the launch of the Greek Chronicle and Greek Telegraph. Although Byron and Stanhope did not always agree with each other, both were key to the publication of the first Greek newspapers. When Stanhope accused Byron of being the enemy of the liberty of the press, he was quick to respond:

"And yet without my money, where would your Greek newspaper be?... Judge me by my actions, not by my words." (Byron)

Byron was named Commander-in-Chief of the allied forces and saw himself standing shoulder to shoulder with Mavrokordatos - as a military leader should war commence, and unquestionably, a political leader.

"The poet had now laid down his pen – and mounted the warrior's plume."

Effectively, Byron had reinvented himself as a Political Statesman of the New Age. He nevertheless remained sceptical regarding his own abilities and the likely impact of the warring Greeks. A new working relationship was established with Mavrokordatos.

"He desires to be of service in whatever way the Government orders him; 'no danger' he says and 'no obstacle will prevent me from hastening whatever the Government orders me'. The man has the greatest disposition to appear useful in our affairs; he is ready to do anything, so long as he knows it is to be of use." (Mavrokordatos)

The Greeks had looked to recapture the Lepanto garrison. Byron agreed to provide for 500 Souliotes and, with a further 100 paid for by the government, he formed his own artillery corps.

On January 21st Missolonghi was again blockaded by Turkish ships of War. On January 22nd, it was Lord Byron's birthday. He wrote a poem which spoke openly of his desire for military glory and the possibility of losing his life:
On this day I complete my thirty_sixth year.

> "My days are in the yellow leaf;
> The flowers and fruits of love are gone;
> The worm, the canker, and the grief
>   Are mine alone!"

> "The sword, the banner, and the field,
> Glory and Greece, around me see!
> The Spartan, borne upon his shield,
>   Was not more free."

> "Seek out - less often sought than found,
> A soldier's grave - for thee the best;
> Then look around, and choose thy ground,
>   And take thy rest."

The ship with William Parry and the stores sent by the London Greek Committee, had been detained in Malta and Corfu. In February, William Parry finally arrived with eight mechanics and four (volunteer) officers. Parry was a 'firemaster' charged with the preparation of Congreve rockets and other weaponry. An old seraglio was converted into a laboratory and an arsenal. Parry prepared a plan for improving the defence of Missolonghi and its harbour. However, finances were not available and work came to a standstill. The two loans from the Greek Committee did not arrive until later in 1824 and in 1825.

With time to spare, Parry joined the Byron Souliote Brigade and was appointed commander of the artillery brigade. He was a somewhat uneducated shipwright, but Byron liked his straightforward attitude and sense of humour. A mutiny amongst the German officers and outrageous demands for higher pay by the Souliotes, caused Byron to disband his corps. The mission to Lepanto was postponed indefinitely when Byron ordered that all agreements between him and the Souliotes were null and void.

Subsequently he set up a new corps with Parry as Commandant with the title of Major. Parry remained faithful to Byron until the very end. In the weeks before Byron's death, he became a close friend, confidante and carer.

Despite both being commissioners from the London Greek Committee, Leicester Stanhope and George Byron often held different views and looked to follow different courses. Stanhope had become an admirer of Odysseas Androutsos - the war lord based in the Acropolis. In March, he left Missolonghi to join him. Anticipating the arrival of a large Turkish force, Odysseas planned a Congress at Salona to discuss the unification of Eastern and Western Greece and examine the best means of defence. Byron had intended to attend the Congress. However, on April 1st 1824, a second Civil War broke out.

At this point, Byron was forced to abandon all hope of achieving his aims and suffered from long-lasting depression.

"He was not prepared to meet with black-hearted treachery; or to see Greeks themselves conspire against their own country. The volcanic mind of Lord Byron was thrown by these events into a violent state of commotion." (Dr.Millingen)

15. THE LAST FEW MONTHS OF LORD BYRON'S LIFE

Here I have focused upon the eye-witness accounts by William Parry and Count Pietro Gamba. Although they agreed on the overall course of events, they did not always agree on the precise day when significant events occurred. We have both the medical reports by his doctors - Francesco Bruno and Julius Millingen, and assessments by 2024 consultants. I hope this will give us an interesting, and hopefully viable insight into the last few months of Byron's life and the cause of his premature death.

Byron playing with his Newfoundland dog, Lyon, amongst his Souliot soldiers. An illustration in William Parry's book 'The last days of Lord Byron.'

Fig 42
Illustration by Robert Seymour (1825)

Both the physicians who attended Byron were young and inexperienced. Francesco Bruno boarded the brig Hercules in Genoa as Byron's personal physician. He had recently qualified at the University of Genoa. He was devoted to Byron and with him to the end. He attended his funeral at Hucknall Torkard and refused to accept payment for his services. Julius Millingen, only twenty-three years of age, had qualified in Edinburgh in 1821. He joined the medical team in April and was with Byron until his death.

February 15th: Byron had been forced to abandon the mission to Lepanto due to the dissension amongst the Souliotes and their constant demands for more pay. He had not been able to ride for some days due to the weather. At 7.00 in the evening, Pietro Gamba discovered Byron lying on a sofa and calling out that he was not well. Later in the evening, with the doctors in attendance, Byron had 'a fit'. This lasted approximately three minutes. He complained of pain in his knee and could not walk. His features were distorted and he was unable to speak (but did not lose his senses).

"I had a strong shock of a convulsive description but whether Epileptic – Paralytic or Apoplectic is not yet decided by the two medical men that attend me. I was speechless with the features much distorted - but not foaming at the mouth - and my struggles so violent that Mr Parry and my servant Tita the Chasseur could not hold me." (Byron)

He was carried upstairs to his bed, at which point he still felt weak, but his features were no longer distorted. He asked if the attack was likely to prove fatal. Pietro Gamba's opinion was that the fit had been brought on principally by recent vexations and his lifestyle. He ate nothing but fish, cheese, vegetables and fruit. He had taken little or no exercise.

February 16th: Byron was out of bed at midday - still very pale and weak. The doctors agreed to bleed him and applied eight leeches to his forehead. Excessive bleeding occurred as the leeches had been placed too close to the temporal artery and caused him to faint. Byron made a slow recovery.

February 22nd: There was a slight recurrence of the attack along with convulsions in the right leg. It quickly settled and he was able to resume his long daily rides. His health visibly improved. He continued to starve himself of 'healthy' food, however, eating only small portions of cheese, fish, vegetables and bread. He was often gloomy and melancholy and he took to playing practical jokes on members of his entourage - which were often unkind.

According to Parry, when in good health, Byron kept to a rigid daily routine:

09.00: he rode out accompanied by his bodyguard and servants

10.00: breakfast - he drank black tea / no sugar and ate dry toast and watercress

Parry received his orders for the day; Byron checked the accounts and dealt with correspondence with Pietro Gamba

Depending on the weather, Byron would ride again or shoot at a mark with pistols

15.00: main meal - vegetarian or vegan

16.00: business meetings with Mavrokordatos, Primates of Missolonghi etc.

After dinner he was involved in the drilling of officers of his corps.

In the evening he conversed with friends and often studied military tactics

23.00: He retired - but did not always choose to sleep. He would read or write, and did not often sleep longer than five hours.

The heavy rains had meant that Byron was no longer able to enjoy his riding out - although evening exercises and drills continued. *"The idea of having so efficient a corps to bring into the field, formed under his own eye, and chiefly at his expense, delighted Lord Byron beyond measure. The hopes which he entertained that the corps would perform some brilliant and distinguished service, gaining him reputation, both as a commander and a statesman."(William Parry : The Last Days of Lord Byron)*

However, his health had not fully recovered and he often complained of slight pains in the head, shivering fits, confusion of thoughts and vision issues. He refused Parry's advice to eat better food and the doctor's advice to bleed him.

"He ate very sparingly and what he did eat was neither nourishing, nor heating… nor blood-making food." (William Parry : The Last Days of Lord Byron)

At the beginning of April, it rained incessantly in Missolonghi and, as a result, the town was cut off from the rest of Greece. Byron was cooped up indoors with little to do. This resulted in more extreme mood swings. It was apparent that he was in poor health and had never really recovered from the convulsive episode he had experienced back in February.

April 9th: Byron received letters from Augusta and John Cam Hobhouse, along with a letter from the Greek Committee which informed him that the loan had finally been negotiated.

His spirits somewhat raised and suffering from claustrophobia due to the bad weather, Byron went out riding with Pietro Gamba. Three miles from the town, they were caught in a severe downpour of rain and remained cold and soaked for several hours. Byron was rowed across the marsh in an open boat in order to reach the house. Two hours after his return home, he shivered uncontrollably and collapsed on the sofa, restless and melancholy. The medical men proposed bleeding, but Byron refused.

"Have you no other remedy than bleeding?_there are many more die of the lancet than the lance." (Byron)

He recalled the prediction of the soothsayer consulted by his mother when he was a young boy: 'beware his thirty-seventh year'. This was said repeatedly to Dr. Julius Millingen on various occasions.

April 10th: Overnight Byron had been feverish. This did not stop him from riding the next morning. By the evening, the fever returned (shuddering, chills and sweats) and Byron complained of 'wandering' pains over his body.

Conversely, Pietro Gamba reported that while he was able to transact business that day - he did not leave the house.

April 11th: Byron resolved to ride out an hour earlier than usual in order to avoid the worst of the weather. Byron spoke much and appeared in good spirits. (Pietro Gamba)

Both physicians recommended bleeding but were met with outright refusal. Instead they dosed him with the likes of castor oil and epsom salts - and encouraged him to have a hot bath.

April 12th: Byron felt worse and kept to his bed with an attack of rheumatic fever. It was thought that riding a horse with a wet saddle may have been a contributory factor.

"Lord Byron's health appeared not thoroughly re-established and he frequently complained of slight pains in the head, shivering fits, confusion of thoughts and visionary fears, all of which inclined to me increasing debility." (William Parry : The Last Days of Lord Byron)

On either the 11th (according to Parry) or the 12th (according to Gamba), Parry and Fletcher tried to persuade Byron to return to Zante for medical advice from a more experienced doctor and to recuperate. Byron proved reluctant to leave Greece, but agreed in principle to the proposed plan.

"I cannot quit Greece while there is still a chance of my being of any utility… While I can stand at all I must stand by The Cause." (Byron)

Preparations were abandoned when a hurricane (most probably the Sirocco), blew in and the countryside was flooded. Vessels were no longer able to sail. Byron refused to be bled once again.

April 13th: Byron rose from his bed but did not leave the house. The fever appeared to have diminished, but pains in his bones and head continued. He was very melancholy and irritable.

April 14th: The fever was less apparent but Byron appeared weak and was dissuaded from riding. He got out of bed at noon.

Gamba felt that the fever was under control and there was no suspicion of danger but Parry noted that Byron's mind frequently wandered in delirium. He was certainly irritated by the doctors' repeated request to bleed him. More purgatives, enemas, castor oil, epsom salts etc. were administered instead.

April 15th: During the day, the fever was still upon him but the pains had gone and he transacted business and received many letters (Pietro Gamba).

In the evening - Byron was seriously ill, mentally confused and occasionally delirious. He suffered a spasmodic bout of coughing, nausea and vomiting (William Parry).

April 16th: Byron again refused to be bled and was warned that the disease might act on the cerebral and nervous system. The doctors made it clear that they would not be held responsible for the consequences. Byron finally succumbed to being bled:

"Come; you are, I see, a damned set of butchers. Take away as much blood as you will; but have done with it." (Byron)

Blood was drawn on two separate occasions. The blood appeared 'very thin in appearance.'

Pietro Gamba did not see Byron on April 16th as he was confined to bed with a sprained ankle.

April 17th: During the night, the fever worsened and Byron talked wildly in delirium. More blood was removed. The doctors called in Dr. Treiber (Byron's artillery brigade) and Dr Loukas Vagias (Mavrocordatos' physician). Together they concluded that the patient was too weak to be bled again. They gave him some Peruvian bark and applied two blistering plasters (counter-irritants) to the inside of his thighs. During the night, the fever progressed, with spasms and convulsions. In a state of delirium, his speech proved more incoherent and rambling.

April 18th: The doctors reported that Byron was delirious and 'alarmingly ill'. There appeared to be inflammation of the brain. More leeches were applied and yet more blood extracted.

Gamba arrived at mid-day. He felt that Byron was able to comprehend a letter from England informing him that the loan had been agreed. Later in the day he became delirious again. The doctors gave him an enema of senna, epsom salts and castor oil.

Byron rose during the afternoon and this proved to be the last time he left his bed. After reading for a few minutes, he returned to his bed. He was delirious and talking wildly about close friends and family. Dr. Bruno and Dr. Milligen became more alarmed and called in Dr. Trieber and Dr Vaya. Following the consultation, Byron appeared to be aware that the end was nigh.

William Fletcher left the room in tears and Tita Falcieri held his hand. Barely able to recognise people, Lord Byron sank into a prolonged state of deep unconsciousness, and never recovered.

April 19th: Twenty-four hours later, at around 6.15 in the evening, Lord George Byron was seen to open his eyes, and immediately shut them again. He died at the age of thirty-six, the type of tragic death he had hoped to avoid - *"not on the field of glory, but on the bed of disease."*

There is much debate concerning the exact last words of Lord Byron. On the 18th, Pietro Gamba heard Byron refer to Greece:

"I have given her my time, my means, my health, - and now I give her my life! - what could I do more."

Around six o'clock in the evening William Fletcher heard him say - "I want to go to sleep now."

On his deathbed cared for by William Parry and Tita Falcieri - having agreed to being bled.

Fig 43
Book illustration by Robert Seymour

The medical opinion in 1824

Recorded by Dr. Julius Millingen:
"His health had suffered previously very much in consequence of the convulsive fits he felt in Feby last, but the immediate cause of his death was a rheumatic fever which attacked him from getting wet in a shower."
"The fever was at its outset very strong, and bleeding was proposed, but he obstinately refused to listen to the urgent remonstrances, and entreaties both of his physician and mine, till the brain was attacked... his answer to all our arguments was "the lancet has killed more than the lance."

Other contemporaries may have seen Byron's death as a combination of factors which impacted upon his physical and mental state:
" 'The wide-eyed idealist' had transformed himself into a 'pragmatic war-leader,' undone by the factionalism of his associates and the incompetence of his physicians; a great hearted mechanic and heroic aristocrat." (William Parry)

View from Lord Byron's House at Missolonghi where he died.

Fig 44
by H.Raper

The Medical Opinion in 2024

After the convulsive episode in February, it was apparent that Byron struggled with his health and never fully recovered - either his health or his spirits. It is unlikely however, that the two earlier events, in August 1823 and February 1824, were directly associated with the illness that started on April 9th. They were more likely to have been epileptic attacks.

Treatment in 1824 commonly involved a combination of bleeding, stimulants, sedatives, purgatives and emetics. Bleeding was very much in fashion. It is likely therefore, that the cause of death was exsanguination (a severe loss of blood) combined with a re-infection of malaria - likely human cerebral malaria (HCM). In support of this diagnosis was the volume of blood removed over the period of his illness (over 40%) and the relapsing bouts of fever in Byron's history. The symptoms provide a consistent explanation - sweats, shaking chills, body aches, fatigue, headaches, delirium, nausea and vomiting.

In Byron's day, malaria was a serious problem and endemic in many parts of Greece - notably Missolonghi. Plasmodium Falciparum malaria was rife in the early 19th century. It is the only one out of the four types of malaria to affect the brain.
The only other possibility that has been raised is Neurosyphilis - the infection of the central nervous system in a patient with syphilis.

"Of the purity of his intentions, and the intenseness of his zeal, the dangers he encountered, the privations he submitted to, the time and money he bestowed, and the life he forfeited, there are such proofs as no other man in this age and country has given." (William Parry : The Last Days of Lord Byron)

16. THE AFTERMATH OF HIS DEATH

Having heard of Byron's death, Trelawny arrived back in Missolonghi having attended the Congress at Salona. He visited the house and exclaimed:
"For three months his house had been besieged, day and night, like a bank that has a run upon it. Now that death had closed the door, it was as silent as a cemetery." (John Trelawny)

The Primates of Missolonghi suspended the Easter Festival, ordering the closure of shops and public offices and twenty-one days of mourning. Thirty-seven guns were fired from the Battery - one for each year of Lord Byron's short life. A funeral was held on April 22nd in the Church of Ayios Nikolaos in Missolonghi. The coffin was of plain wood and surmounted by Byron's helmet and sword(s).
Byron's organs had been removed and placed in separate urns so that his lungs and larynx or his heart could remain in Greece.
The simple ceremony reflected the fact that they had wanted Byron to be formally buried in Missolonghi or the Temple of Theseus on the hill of the Acropolis in Athens. Byron had also looked to be buried abroad:
"I trust they won't think of 'pickling', and bringing me home to Clod or Blunderbuss Hall. I'm sure my bones would not rest in an English grave, or my clay mix with the earth of that country. I believe the thought would drive me mad on my death bed." (Byron 1819)

His coffin was put on the brig Florida, accompanied by William Fletcher, Tita Falcieri, Lega Zambelli, Dr Bruno, Benjamin Lewis - plus a guard of Greek soldiers and Lyon, his faithful dog.
News of Byron's death was published on the front page of The Times. Byron had worked on his memoirs at various times throughout his lifetime. In 1819 Thomas Moore had visited Byron in Venice. Byron presented him with 78 folio pages of his memoirs.

He had stipulated that they were not to be published in his lifetime. Moore sold them to John Murray. John Cam Hobhouse and John Murray both felt strongly that memoirs recounting Byron's life, loves and opinions should be destroyed. Together, Hobhouse and Murray along with Thomas Moore, Augusta Leigh and Lady Byron's representatives, burnt the only copy of Byron's memoirs in the grate of John Murray's drawing room in Albemarle Street, London. Within minutes his memoirs were reduced to a mound of ashes.

His friends had envisaged a triumphant public burial in Westminster Abbey or St Paul's Cathedral. Both adamantly refused him.

Lord Byron's body was interred in the family vault at the Church of St Mary Magdalene in Hucknall Torkard, Nottinghamshire
Fig 45
Interior of St Mary Magdalene Marble slab above the grave donated by the King of Greece

Byron had previously stated that he wished to be buried at Newstead Abbey in the tomb alongside his dog Boatswain.
"I desire that me body be buried in the Vault in the garden of Newstead without any ceremony or burial service whatever and that no inscription over my name and age shall be written on the Tomb or Tablet and it is my will that my faithful dog not be removed from the said vault." (Byron's wills in 1811 and 1815)

The neoclassical sculptor Bertel Thorvaldsen had been commissioned to turn his 1816 bust of Lord Byron into a full length statue – intended by Hobhouse for Westminster Abbey.

Having been refused by the Dean, it was eventually placed in the Wren Library at Trinity College where it now stands proudly representing 'The genius of poetry'. Only in 1969 did the Abbey finally agree to memorialise and commemorate Byron with a simple white marble stone in the floor alongside Dylan Thomas, Lewis Carroll and D.H. Lawrence.

Byron's body was transported to London, and laid in state for two days at 20 Great George Street, Westminster. The route was lined with crowds as the coffin was taken in a horse-drawn carriage to Nottinghamshire. On July 16th 1824, the funeral was held at St Mary Magdalene Church and the coffin placed in the family vault. *"Buried like a nobleman – since we could not bury him as a poet."* *(Hobhouse)*

The vault was opened 114 years later in 1938 and three tiers of coffins were identified – Lord George Byron, his mother and daughter Ada, Countess of Lovelace.

What happened to Byron's friends and servants:

John Cam Hobhouse - MP for Westminster; married with three daughters. A formidable politician, he fought constantly on behalf of the poor and child labour. He was given a knighthood and elevated to the House of Lords - 1st Baron Broughton.
William Fletcher - in partnership with Lega Zambelli, they opened Macaroni – a pasta manufacturing business in London.
Giovanni Battista Falcieri (Tita) - returned to the war and was employed by Benjamin Disraeli. He returned to Buckinghamshire with Disraeli and married Disreali's wife's maid.
William Parry - wrote and published his book 'The last days of Lord Byron.' Trelawney claimed that he "drank himself into a

madhouse." He spent the last years of his life in a lunatic asylum where he died at the age of eighty-five.

Mary Shelley - returned to England a year later and devoted her time to the upbringing of her son, Percy Florence Shelley, and her career as a writer. She refused offers of marriage and lived a relatively meagre existence.

Teresa Guiccoli - after his death, Teresa wrote a biographical account of Lord Byron's life in Italy. She became the lover of Henry Edward Fox, 3rd Lord Holland and subsequently married the Marquis de Boissy. When she died with no children, her papers were inherited by her grand-nephew. He hid them away believing his great aunt's scandalous relationship with Lord Byron would damage the Gamba family reputation. The book was not published until 2005.

Pietro Gamba - Byron's companion and devotee, brought all Byron's personal papers back to John Cam Hobhouse in England. He then returned to Missolonghi to fight. He died of typhus fever at the age of twenty-five.

Edward John Trelawny - married Odysseas Androutsos's thirteen year old sister. Having survived an assassination attempt, he returned to England without her. He later published his 'Recollections of the Last Days of Shelley and Byron' and 'Records of Shelley Byron and the Author.' He lived a long successful life and remained active into his eighties.

Dr. Julius Michael Millingen - served as a surgeon in the Greek army. He later moved to Constantinople as court physician to five consecutive Sultans.

17. BYRON'S WAR LEGACY

Philhellenism appeared at the start of the Greek War in 1821. Supportive organisations across Europe and America were formed and members were largely intellectuals and lovers of antiquity. Lord Byron, with his poetry, his liberal ideology, his arrival in Greece with financial support and his untimely death in 1824, became a symbol of Philhellenism. His death played a crucial part in motivating the union of Greek factions against the Ottoman Empire and the increased involvement of western nations.

Byron is remembered as generous and brave - *'A hero' 'A saviour' 'A deliverer'*.
"Nothing can be more serviceable to the cause than all you have done. I can only trust that the great sacrifices which you have made will contribute to the final success of the great cause of the independence of Greece. This will indeed be worth living for and will make your name and character stand far above any contemporary." (John Cam Hobhouse)

During the premiership in Britain of philhellene George Canning, the first intervention of the Great Powers took place. Britain, France and Russia signed the Convention of London in 1827. This provided for a cease-fire and Greek autonomy. The Ottomans refused to agree. As a result, the allied forces blockaded the coasts of the Peloponnese. The Turkish Egyptian fleet was annihilated at the naval battle of Navarino in 1827. In 1830, the founding of the Modern Greek State was recognised by the Great Powers. Ioannis Kapodistrias was elected by the Third National Assembly of Troizene. He was murdered in 1831, and the following year saw the creation of the Kingdom of Greece and the election of Otto of Bavaria as king.

Timeline following Lord Byron's death (1825 - 1832)

1825

April: The Fall of Missolonghi. The Ottoman forces had failed to capture the city in 1822 and 1823. They returned in 1825, led by Kioutahi Pasha and Ibrahim Pasha of Egypt. The Greeks held out for nearly a year before they ran out of food. They attempted a mass breakout in April 1826, and only a small number survived. This moving event had a profound effect internationally. It proved a key factor which led to the intervention by the Great Powers, who by then, felt ever more sympathy for the Greek Cause.

May: Battle of Maniaki. Ottoman Egyptian forces defeated the Greek forces. Grigorios Papaflessas (Greek priest and government official) and Pieros Voidis (military leader) were killed in action.

1826

November: Church of Agios Georgios, Arachova - one of the most decisive moments in the history of the war. Ottoman forces under the command of Mustafa Bey were defeated by the Greek forces led by Georgios Karaiskakis. Fighting took place around the church and the battle lasted six days.

Frank Abney Hastings, British Naval officer and benefactor of the Hellenic Navy, had realised that the Greeks in sailing ships were likely to be defeated without steam ships at their disposal. Back in an English shipyard, he used his own money to construct the Karteria (Perseverance) and design state of the art military equipment. The Karteria was the first steam-powered warship in history to be used in combat operations. It arrived in Nafplio in December 1826.

1827

September: Battle of Itea in the Gulf of Corinth. A small Greek squadron commanded by Frank Abney Hastings launched a raid on an Ottoman fleet. The steam-powered warship Karteria played a crucial part in the Greek victory.

October: Battle of Navarino Bay on the Peloponnese peninsula in the Ionian Sea. Allied forces from Britain, France and Russia defeated Ottoman and Egyptian forces.

1828

January: Count Ioannis Kapodistrias was elected the first head of state of an independent Greece. He served as governor of Greece between 1828 and 1831.

1830

February: The London Protocol treaty was signed by France, Russia and Great Britain. It was the first official international act that recognized Greece as a sovereign and independent state.

1831

September: Ioannis Kapodistrias was assassinated on his way to the church of St Spyridon in Nafplio.

1832

July: The International London Conference was convened to establish a stable government. Seventeen-year-old Prince Otto of Bavaria, was crowned King of Greece. The Kingdom of Greece was ratified in the Treaty of Constantinople, whereby the sultan formally recognised Greek Independence.

Byron's actions also inspired other poets to adopt a political stance. Notably Alexander Pushkin, who in his poems, expressed sympathy for victims of oppression and inequality. He was banished from St Petersburg for publishing poems of political dissent notably, *Ode to Liberty*.

18. BYRON'S LITERARY LEGACY AND RECOGNITION

Byron continues to captivate readers with his passionate and controversial works. He was widely seen as a Romantic poet and satirist whose poetry captured the imagination of Europe and America.

"I am also told of considerable literary honours in Germany - Goethe I am told is my professed patron and protector. Goethe and the Germans are particularly fond on Don Juan - which they judge of as a work of Art." (Byron - Letter to John Murray 1822)

18a. The Byronic Hero

The characterisation of The Byronic hero originated with Lord Byron in his poem *Childe Harold's Pilgrimage* - followed by such works as *Manfred*, *Don Juan* and *The Corsair*.

Tall dark and handsome; wild and glamorous
Romantic but unfaithful
Intelligent, egotistical, ambitious, argumentative
Strongly self-aware and sentimental
Hypersensitive and quick to take offence
Weighed down by his actions and self-destructive
Never content and always yearning for new sensations

An outcast - holding contradictory beliefs to the norm
A rebel - on the side of the people and opposed to the Establishment
A protagonist - wanting to do good but unclear how to achieve his goal

The Byronic Hero is represented throughout Western literature and entertainment to this day.

Some Recognisable Literary Byronic heroes
Sherlock Holmes by Arthur Conan Doyle -
intelligent, self-destructive, arrogant
Edward Dantes in the Count of Monte Cristo by Alexander Dumas -
superior intelligence
Heathcliff in Wuthering Heights by Emily Bronte -
hints of incest between Heathcliff and Catherine
Mr Rochester in Jane Eyre by Charlotte Bronte -
past sexual transgressions and doomed marriage
Damon Salvatore in The Vampire Diaries by L.T. Smith
Severus Snape in Harry Potter by J.K. Rowling

… and the Superheroes of Marvel Comics - namely Loki in Where
Mischief Lies, Wolverine and Batman

In plays, musicals and film:
Rick Blaine in Casablanca
Erik in Phantom of the Opera
Bram Stoker's Dracula (Francis Ford Coppola)
Captain Jack Sparrow in Pirates of the Caribbean
Edward Cullen in Twilight

Some will say that the ultimate Byronic Superhero is indeed
Batman:
- Highly intelligent but violent and self-destructive
- A brooding and haunted figure forced to deal with the traumas in
his life
- A tendency to rebel against authority

18b. Commemorative Poetry

The Hero of Missolonghi

Dionysios Solomos had been influenced by Byron's brand of European Romanticism and was one of the first poets to respond to the death of Lord Byron.

"Liberty, cease for a moment
Striking hard with your sword;
Now approach here to lament
By the body of this noble lord;"

In 1824, he wrote his personal eulogy, *'Lyrical Poem on the Death of Lord Byron'*. He identified Byron as 'an artist' 'a liberal' and 'an idealist'.

Andreas Kalvos wrote his ode to Byron in 'Lyre - Odes of Andreas Calvos', where he famously referred to Byron as 'The Britannic Muse'. Having expressed sorrow over his death, he expressed the admiration that Greeks and civilised nations had for Byron.

"Oh Byron, exquisite spirit,
Offspring of the Brittanic
Muses and unfortunate
Friend of glorious Greece."

"Greece in gratitude
Is seeking to crown you
As a noble friend
As her comforter,
Her benefactor."

A generation later, Greek poets focussed on commemorative poetry and their admiration for the 'Philhellenic Englishman'. Proveleggios had felt strongly that Byron's body should have been buried in Greece - his 'Immortal Country'.

"If the force of your singing in the future does expire,
And is drowned in the ocean of the years that transpire,
The memory of the fighter for freedom shall remain
In Greecian hearts indelibly engraved with pain."

The centennial of Byron's death rekindled interest and inspiration. It focused on the two very different aspects of 'The Warrior Poet'. In the words of Kostis Palamas:

"You haven't come with your song's attractive ire;
you came bringing your life to a holy sacrifice in an altar fire;
if you lived like Dionysius, you passed as a Messiah."

… and Sotiris Skipis:

"One hundred years passed as if it were yesterday,
and one thousand it will be the same;
And the Greeks, immortal bard, then like today,
will be singing of your fame."

Many of us 'Byromaniacs', would love to see the same rekindling of interest and inspiration in response to the bicentennial of Lord Byron's death in 2024.
"Byron was a rock star of his day, a prototype for the contemporary celebrity. His fans were called 'Byromaniacs' and they wrote him HUNDREDS of letters every day." (BBC Radio 4)

19. CLOSE FRIENDS, COLLEAGUES AND TRAVEL COMPANIONS
Their origins and influences on Byron

1798-1805
Nottinghamshire and Newstead Abbey

On inheriting Newstead Abbey at the age of ten, Byron became a ward of the Court of Chancery with three Guardians – his mother, John Hanson (solicitor and quasi-father figure) and Frederick 5th Earl of Carlisle (cousin). The latter consulted with Hanson on issues regarding education and used his influence to obtain an initial sum of £300 from the Civil List for Mrs Byron.

It was to John Hanson that the eleven year old boy wrote, regarding his nurse May Gray. She had accompanied him to Nottingham to help care for his foot. Byron informed Hanson that she had been in the habit of coming into his bed and engaging in sexual activities with him. After she had been drinking, she would beat him. May Gray was eventually dismissed in 1799.

"Since you are going to Newstead I beg if you meet Gray send her a packing as fast as possible." (Letter to John Hanson 1799)

Southwell and Burgage Manor

Catherine Byron rented Burgage Manor on a seven year lease. Byron and his mother were based in Southwell until she went to live at Newstead Abbey in 1809.

Elizabeth Bridget Pigot (1783-1866) - lived opposite Byron in Southwell. She was like an elder sister to the young Byron and encouraged his poetic ambitions. Along with her brother **John Pigot**, they became Byron's close confidants. Elizabeth copied many of his rough drafts and encouraged him to write his first volume of poetry, *Fugitive Pieces*.

"Few people understood Byron. Some mistook his reserve and silence for pride or superiority, but I knew he naturally had a kind and feeling heart and there was not a single spark of malice in him." (John Pigott)

Initially Byron disliked Southwell – *"No society except old parsons and old maids."* His opinion mellowed, largely through his friendship with the Pigot family:

"My time has been much lately occupied with very different pursuits - performing in private theatricals - publishing a volume of poems (at the request of my friends for their perusal) - making love - and taking physic." (Letter to the Earl of Clare 1807)

Harrow School 1801-1805

It is important here to bear in mind that 'fagging' was a traditional practice in British public schools. Younger pupils were required to act as personal servants to the eldest boys. The senior (fag-master) was responsible for their general behaviour and wellbeing. He protected his fags from bullying and abuse. A fag's duties would include humble tasks such as blacking boots, brushing clothes and running errands.

John FitzGibbon 2nd Earl of Clare (1792-1851)

An Anglo Irish aristocrat and close school friend, Byron described him as his *"earliest and dearest friend."* He claimed to love him 'ad infinitum' such that he could never hear the word 'Clare' without feeling a 'murmur of the heart.'

Active in the House of Lords, he was later appointed Governor of Bombay and finally in later life, Lord Lieutenant of the City of Limerick in Southern Ireland.

George Sackville-West 5th Earl De La Warr (1791-1869)

A younger pupil at Harrow School, admired by Byron as *"the most good tempered, amiable, clever fellow in the universe… and remarkably handsome."*

A British courtier and Tory politician, he later served as Lord
Chamberlain of the Household and member of the Privy Council.

John Thomas Claridge (1792-1868)

Claridge attended Harrow School in 1805, the same year that Byron
graduated. Byron continued to visit Harrow, staying with Henry
Drury who shared accommodation with Claridge. The latter
expressed his love for Byron and stayed at Newstead Abbey in 1809.
Returning from his travels, Byron renewed their friendship, but
found his company 'dull' and 'boring'.

John Wingfield (1791-1811)

Byron's schoolmate at Harrow. He served with the Coldstream
Guards at the battle of Waterloo and rose to become a Lieutenant
Colonel in the British army. Byron was clearly upset by his early
death at the age of only twenty.

Edward Noel Long (1788-1809)

Byron's classmate at Harrow and fellow student at Cambridge.

Trinity College Cambridge (1805-1808)

Byron had initially expressed a preference for Oxford University - but
was well content to be going up to Trinity College Cambridge.
*"My companions were not unsocial but the contrary - lively -
hospitable - of rank & fortune - & gay far beyond my gaiety."* (Byron)

Edward Noel Long (1788-1809)

Byron's classmate at Harrow School, their friendship continued
throughout their time at University. They went on long swims and
rides as well as reading and talking together. Both feared becoming
overweight and this proved to be the beginning of Byron's thinning
regimes. They were very close friends and he was the subject of one
of Byron's early poems in Hours of Idleness 1807.
He became an ensign in the Coldstream Guards and died at sea
during the Peninsular War at the age of only twenty-one.

John Cam Hobhouse (1786-1869)

Founder of the Whig Club and Amicable Society and writer of verse. 'Hobby' was perceived as Byron's faithful friend and 'bulldog'. His radical opinions helped Byron establish his own political beliefs. John Cam Hobhouse became a friend for life accompanying Byron on his travels.

" He was a cheerful companion, full of odd and droll stories, which he told extremely well; he was also good humoured and intelligent - altogether an advantageous specimen of a well-educated English gentleman." (John Galt in Caligari, Sardinia)

'Hobby' was described by Byron as *"my best and dearest friend."* He often warned Byron regarding his choice of women and works of literature.

Fig 46
John Cam Hobhouse
1st Baron Broughton
Engraving by J.Hopwood 1834
Published by J Murray

Pietro Gamba dedicated his Journal of 1825 to John Cam Hobhouse MP for Westminster:
"You are Lord Byron's oldest and dearest friend; you were the companion of his Lordship's early travels, when he first visited Greece; when the contrast between it's past glory and present

degradation awakened his genius, and lit up in his breast an intense love for that sacred and unhappy country which endured to the last moment of his life."

Their correspondence was often candid and witty - but not always cordial. On some occasions, Byron took note - but on others, Hobhouse's concerns were blatantly ignored.

Fig 47
Letter to Hobhouse

Some examples of friction between Byron and 'Hobby':
Hobhouse strongly recommended that Byron should terminate his relationship with Caroline Lamb. He was shocked by the nature of the relationship and concerned about a potential elopement.

Byron sent his manuscript of *Don Juan* to Hobhouse to read. Hobhouse informed him that, having spoken to others, he felt that Don Juan was 'impossible to publish.' Its content was 'indecent' with personal attacks and mockery of marriage, religion and the establishment. Byron was also offended by a letter Hobhouse wrote to him about *Cain* which he thought would ruin Byron's reputation because of its attack on accepted religious views.

After Byron had moved to Italy, Hobhouse became an important link between the poet and his London publisher.

Scrope Berdmore Davies (1782-!852)

A university friend and heavy gambler. Based on his winnings, he guaranteed the loan, without which Byron would have been forced to delay his Mediterranean Tour.

Scrope followed in Byron's footsteps. He had affairs with Lady Caroline Lamb and Lady Frances Wedderburn Webster. Financial difficulties subsequently forced him into self-exile.

Charles Skinner Mathews (1785-1811)

Founder of the circle of friends who enjoyed diverse sexual exploits. They all spoke and wrote to each other in a Latin code in order to communicate their progress and achievements regarding various relationships. Mathews advocated pederasty in the classic Greek tradition.

John Edleston (1789-1811)

When Byron was seventeen, he met John Edleston, a fifteen year old chorister at Trinity Chapel, Cambridge. While Byron almost certainly had romantic feelings, their brief friendship appeared largely to be based upon romantic, homoerotic desires:

"the youthful idol of unfulfilled desire."
"A violent though pure passion."

In 1806 Edleston gave Byron a cornelian brooch pin in the shape of a heart to which Byron referred to in his poem *'The Adieu'.* He gave the brooch initially to Elizabeth Pigot. Upon the death of Edleston in 1811, Byron wrote to Elizabeth's mother. He explained that Edleston had died and asked for the brooch to be returned to him.

"He offer'd it with downcast look,
As fearful that I might refuse it,
I told him when the gift I took,
My only fear should be to lose it."

George Bryan 'Beau' Brummell (1778-1840)

The high priest of men's fashion and preeminent example of the dandy. He rejected overly ornate clothes in favour of understated but perfectly fitted and tailored bespoke items of clothing. At times, Brummell and Byron used the same tailor.

Mediterranean Tour in 1809

Accompanied by his University friend John Cam Hobhouse and his servants Joe Murray, William Fletcher and Robert Rushton.

Joseph Murray (1737- 1820)

Joe entered the service of the 5th Lord back in the 1760s. He was initially employed as a sailor-boy in the schooners that crossed the Upper Lake at Newstead Abbey.

He was there to welcome the ten year old George Byron on his first visit to the ancestral home. Regarded as Byron's chief servant - he was in many ways a father figure to the young lord.

Fig 48
*Joseph Murray
by Thomas Barber*

He accompanied Byron on many of his early travels abroad. Byron had intended that 'Old Joe' be buried alongside himself and the dog Boatswain in the tomb at Newstead Abbey.

This notion did not appeal to Joe Murray - especially in the absence of his master -

"His lordship might be buried with dogs, but I will be buried with Christians."

William Fletcher (1775-1839)
A farm worker at Newstead Abbey, he was promoted to the position of valet and groom. As Byron's personal assistant, he was with him until his death in Greece.

Robert Rushton (1793-1833)
The son of a tenant farmer and Byron's official page. Closely protected and educated by Byron, he accompanied him on the early part of his Mediterranean Tour. He was sent home prior to visiting the Turkish provinces as Byron considered them to be unsafe. He attended boarding school in Newark, Nottinghamshire.
"Deduct the expenses of education from your rent." (Letter to Mr. Rushton)

Nicolo Giraud (born c.1795)
A student at the Capuchin Monastery in Athens. He became Byron's majordomo and travelling companion. He is speculated to have also been his lover.

Return from Mediterranean Travels 1811 (Age 23)

John Murray (1778-1843)
London publisher, literary critic and adviser to Byron. He also published works by Sir Walter Scott and Jane Austen.

Douglas Kinnaird (1788-1830)
Fellow member of the sub-committee directing affairs at Drury Lane theatre. A close friend, Byron referred to him as *"my trusty and*

trustworthy trustee and banker." He was frequently consulted on business negotiations with John Murray and insisted on the destruction of Byron's memoirs after his death.

Elizabeth Milbanke Lamb (1751-1818)

Viscountess Melbourne was a close friend, confidant and advisor to Lord Byron. She was much older (in her sixties) and influenced him in a variety of ways. She encouraged him to avoid Caroline Lamb, her daughter-in-law, and marry her niece, Annabella Milbanke. *"She was my greatest friend of the female gender … When I say friend I mean not mistress for that's the antipode." (Byron)*

Self - exile
Percy Bysshe Shelley (1792-1822)

Shelley and Byron met at Lake Geneva, Switzerland in 1816. Shelley had been disinherited by his father after he eloped to Scotland to marry his first wife Harriet Westbrook (aged sixteen). He was expelled from University College, Oxford after publishing a pamphlet advocating atheism, entitled *"The Necessity of Atheism".* He went into permanent self-exile two years after Byron in 1818.

Shelley and Byron soon discovered that they had much to share. Shelley was a poet, radical thinker, advocate of free love … and a vegetable diet.

Fig 49
Engraving by William Finden from original portrait by Amelia Curran

"As to poor Shelley, who is another bugbear to you and the world he is, to my knowledge, the least selfish and the mildest of men - a man who had made more sacrifices of his fortune and feelings for others than any I have heard of." (Byron - Letter to Thomas Moore 1822)

Shelley introduced Byron to Alexandros Mavrokordatos in Pisa and encouraged Byron to support the Greek Cause. The death of Shelley in a drowning accident in 1822, aged only twenty-nine, proved a turning point in Byron's life and legacy.

Byron and Shelley were close friends and spoke frequently to each other about their poetry. In this context, it is perhaps not surprising that one poet's work inspired the other. Shelley is regarded as one of the major contributors to English Romantic poetry. Among Shelley's best known works are *Ozymandias, Ode to the West Wind, Prometheus Unbound* and *Adonais.*

Mary Wollstonecraft Shelley (1797-1851)

Best known as the author of the Gothic novel *Frankenstein*; or, *The Modern Prometheu*s. Mary's father William Godwin, had befriended and mentored the young Percy Bysshe Shelley. They met when she was sixteen and he was twenty-one, and fell in love.

Together Shelley and Mary Wollstonecraft eloped to France in 1814 accompanied by Mary's stepsister Claire Clairmont.

Fig 50
*Mary Shelley
by Richard Rothwell 1840*

They married in 1816 when his first wife, Harriet Westbrook, committed suicide. Mary was a writer and her husband's editor. They had four children, but only Percy Florence survived to adulthood and outlived her.

She described Lord Byron as -
"The fascinating – faulty – childish – philosophical being – daring the world – docile to a private circle – impetuous and indolent – gloomy and yet more gay than any other." (Mary Shelley Letter to John Murray)

Pietro Gamba (1801-1827)
An Italian nobleman, freedom fighter and member of the Italian Carbonari, he became acquainted with Lord Byron through his sister Teresa. He quickly became a close companion and, as his second in command, he accompanied Byron to Greece to fight in the Greek War of Independence. In conversation with the Countess of Blessington, Byron said that Pietro was *"One of the most amiable young men he had ever encountered."*

Count Pietro Gamba's Journal, 'A Narrative of Lord Byron's Last Journey to Greece' (Published in 1825) has provided us with a credible and comprehensive source of material pertaining to Byron's commitment to the Greek Cause and to his life and death in Missolonghi.
"I conducted the greater part of his public business, every circumstance of which was communicated to me. I kept a diary, containing a minute account of all the events of the day. Every fact which I narrate may, therefore, be received as authentic." (Pietro Gamba, 1825)

20. BYRON'S SEXUALITY

20a. Background
Discussing Byron's emotional and sexual proclivities is not easy. His sexual orientation has long been a difficult and speculative topic as evidence is often vague, ill-defined or contradictory. Furthermore, previous authors have been reprimanded for alluding to his sexuality and use of the word 'gay'. Once abroad, in self-exile, there is little or no evidence that Byron was attracted to post-adolescent, adult males. Is this a fact? Or was it that he finally understood the importance of discretion and circumspection? Of course, we do not have Byron's final memoirs, which were destroyed by well-meaning friends who felt they would prove to be 'too scandalous to ever see the light of day.'

It is accepted that Byron had 'a robust sex life'. He has been referred to as the 'Casanova of The Romantics' and 'The Rock Star of his day'. In 2024, the modern definitions which seem most appropriate to Byron in a broad geographical context are 'Omnisexual' or 'Queer.' In the early 1800s however, we would have referred to him simply as 'bi-sexual'.

Historically relevant Laws and Moralities
It is important to recognise the law and accepted rules of behaviour in different European countries during Byron's lifetime.

In England
All penetrative homosexual acts committed by men were punishable by death.
The age of consent was 10 for girls and 14 for boys.
Incest was not illegal until The Punishment of Incest Act in 1908. It was however seen as an ecclesiastical offence requiring an act of penance.

In Italy

Most of the areas of Italy had eliminated all criminal and civil laws concerning sodomy. The Napoleonic Code (first enacted in France in 1804) ensured sodomy was legal between consenting adults above the legal age of consent.

Italy attracted a large gay community as, apart from the relaxed laws, Italy was strongly linked with antiquity and opportunities for clandestine meetings were readily identifiable.

The role of Cavalier Servente was commonplace (in the higher echelons of society). In the early 19th century, a Cisbeo was the recognised gallant and lover of his lady. He was a gentleman of equal status normally chosen at the end of the first year of marriage. He attended her everywhere e.g. handed her into the gondola, attended social and literary gatherings, escorted her to the opera and sat next to her at dinner.

"Used in politest circles to express the supernumerary slave who stays close to the lady as part of dress. Her word the only law which he obeys." (Byron)

In Greece

'Greek love' became the euphemism for homosexuality and pederasty. Pederasty was defined as sexual activity involving an older man and a younger male - usually in his teens. The adolescent must have undergone puberty. Such a relationship had enjoyed particular esteem in the ancient world, especially in classical Athens. Byron observed that:

"Pederasty is practised underhandedly by the Greeks and openly carried out by the Turks."

20b. Relationships with Women

England: The early years

Mary Duff - a distant cousin in Aberdeen and object of Byron's affection when he was only eight years old.

"How very odd that I should have been so devotedly fond of that girl, at an age when I could neither feel passion, nor know the meaning of the word and the effect!" (Byron)

Margaret Parker - Byron's first cousin. The emotion between Byron and his cousin was very deep and he was grief-struck by her death following a fall from a horse. At the age of twelve, George Byron wrote his first love poem.

"My first dash into poetry, was as early as 1800 - It was the ebul-lition of a passion for my first cousin Margaret Parker, one of the most beautiful of Evanescent beings.- I have long forgotten the verses - but it would be difficult for me to forget her." (Byron)

Mary Chaworth - Byron's adolescent love when he reached the age of sixteen (and Mary was eighteen). She rejected the *"lame bashful, boy lord"* but remained the inspiration for works such as 'Hills of Annesley' (1805) 'The Adieu' (1807) and 'The Dream' (1816).

> *"Hills of Annesley, Bleak and Barren,*
> *Where my thoughtless Childhood stray'd."*

Augusta Leigh - Byron started corresponding with his half-sister (five years older than himself) in 1804. She was the daughter of his father, John Byron, and Amelia Osborne.

Mediterranean Tour: Italy

Marianna Segati - a Venetian draper's wife renowned for her attractiveness and beautiful singing voice. She proved to be an obliging companion who was able to adapt to Byron's mood swings.

Margarita Cogni - an illiterate baker's wife, she was described as loud and boisterous with a very jealous nature. She left her husband to move in with Byron. When he asked her to leave, she threw herself into the canal.

England: Post Travels

Lady Caroline Lamb - a very public affair commenced in 1812 when Byron was twenty-four years of age (Caroline twenty-six). Right at the start of their relationship, she claimed that *'He was Mad, Bad and Dangerous to Know'*.

Jane Elizabeth Harley Countess of Oxford - fourteen years his senior, she was a friend of Lady Caroline Lamb. She frequently took lovers and her large number of children were known as the 'Harleian Miscellany' due to uncertainties as to whether her husband was the father. Her affairs were considered unacceptable and she had few friends who were prepared to receive her.

Anne Isabella Milbanke - in 1815, Byron (aged twenty-six) married Annabella (aged twenty-two) and declared that he had *"Given up Concubinage"* and was *"Sick of Promiscuity"*. Their daughter Augusta Ada was born the same year and Annabella left her husband less than a year later in January 1816.

Self-exile

Claire Clairmont - Mary Shelley's step sister and Byron's lover. Their illegitimate daughter Clara Allegra Byron was born on 12th January 1817 back in England.

Teresa Gamba Guiccoli - in 1819 Byron was aged thirty-one and Teresa was aged nineteen. They met soon after her wedding to Count Alessandro Guiccoli - a gentleman well advanced in years. Byron was designated Cavalier Servente (Gentleman in Waiting) and lover. She was his final and true love:

"I love you and you love me. - at least you say so, and act as if you did. But I more than love you, and cannot cease to love you." (Byron)

Byron's Choice of Women

Byron's women were often independent minded women who were ahead of the curve when it came to women's rights. They were intelligent, forthright women looking to lead lives considerably richer than their home-based contemporaries. They led lives that were often unconventional.

Mary Ann Chaworth Musters

Distant relatives, they lived on adjacent estates. She was the heiress of Annesley Hall and surrounding lands - within easy riding distance of Newstead Abbey. They met as teenagers in 1803 and Byron, aged fifteen, felt himself deeply in love. He refused to return to Harrow school at the start of the autumn term. Mary famously repelled his advances, and declared that she had no interest in a "lame, bashful, boy lord."

> *"Adieu to sweet Mary for ever!*
> *From her I must quickly depart.*
> *Though the fates us from each other sever,*
> *Still her image will dwell in my heart."*

Two years later she married John ('Jack') Musters of Colwick Hall - a great sportsman, a keen hunter and master of the hounds. He was ten years her senior and a well known philanderer. He became High Sheriff of Nottinghamshire and Lieutenant-Colonel of the 1st regiment of the Nottingham Militia.

Byron looked back on his relationship with Mary Chaworth with sadness and regret; imagining how different his life would have been if he had married the adolescent love of his life.

Fig 51
Mary Ann Chaworth Musters
by Thomas Phillips

"Our union would have healed feuds in which blood had been shed by our fathers - it would have joined lands - broad and rich - it would have joined at least one heart and two persons not ill-matched in years (She is two years my elder) and - and - and - what has been the result? - She has married a man older than herself - been wretched - and separated. - I have married - & am separated. - and yet we are not united." (Byron)

In 1831, Colwick Hall was sacked by rioters and the building was set on fire. Mary hid outside in the rain with her daughter during the night. She died four months later.

Augusta Leigh
A half-sister and trusted confidante. Their love was rooted in childish affections and memories but later developed into a much more serious relationship.

"I never knew what it was to love before. There is a woman I love so passionately." (Byron)

"I am at this moment in a far more serious and entirely new scrape than any of the last months - and that's saying a great deal."
(Byron - Letter to his confidante, Lady Melbourne)

Augusta's romantic feelings for her husband, Lt. Colonel George Leigh, were seriously affected by domestic frictions and debts. Byron is known to have paid off some of her husband's debts.

Lady Caroline Lamb
The daughter of the Earl of Bessborough and Henrietta Ponsonby, she was a tomboy as a child and her spirit of recklessness became ingrained. She had little formal education. She was, however, intelligent and witty, and wrote poetry and prose. Aged nineteen, Caroline married William Lamb in 1805. He was the son of Lord Melbourne and they resided at Melbourne House.

Initially Byron identified some appealing characteristics – an inquisitive mind, a penchant for good literature and a common interest in politics. She was vivacious and flirtatious and clearly attracted to intellectual men. They met in 1812 and embarked upon a tumultuous affair. Byron led her to believe he loved her. On his part, the relationship tended more to reflect his obsession with the pursuit of a woman, followed by a period of ennui and irritation. She was not however easy to ignore.

As a result of *Childe Harold's Pilgrimage*, Byron achieved fame and celebrity status overnight. On reading his poetry, Lady Caroline sought to meet the author. She was quick to claim that he was *"Mad, Bad and Dangerous to know."*

Fig 52
Lady Caroline Lamb
Engraving by Henry Meyer

Caroline was hurt by his rejection and her husband took her to Ireland to recover from the shock. Once back in England she continued to make very public advances to win Byron back.

Her scandalous book *Glenarvon* contributed to Byron's notoricty. It was a Gothic novel which caricatured her friend Jane Harley, Countess of Oxford with whom Byron had an affair. In her book she copied a letter she claimed to have received from Byron:
"I am no longer your lover; and since you oblige me to confess it, by this truely unfeminine persecution, - learn, that I am attached to another…

I shall ever continue your friend, if your Ladyship will permit me to style myself; and as a first proof of my regard, I offer this advice, correct your vanity which is ridiculous; exert your absurd caprices upon others; and leave me in peace." (Byron)

Anne Isabella (a.k.a. Annabella) Milbanke

Annabella had become friendly with Caroline Lamb and saw Byron for the first time at one of her morning parties. She refused Byron's initial proposal in 1812, but resumed contact at a time when Byron felt it was time to marry and was feeling out of spirits.

"I do believe that to marry would be my wisest step. I have no heart to spare and expect none in return." (Byron)

Byron, typical of his ancestors, was strapped for cash. As an only child with expectations from her childless uncle, Lord Wentworth, Annabella did not lack suitors. Their married life lasted almost exactly one year. Her belief that she could change him proved ill founded. After the birth of Ada in 1815, Annabella returned to her parents and demanded a legal separation.

Annabella had been in love with her own conception of the author of *Childe Harold* rather than the man himself. She had looked to reform and restore him to the path of righteousness.

Fig 53
*Anne Isabella Noel Byron
Engraving by William Finden*

"She married me from vanity and the hope of reforming me and fixing me." (Byron)

"What an odd situation and friendship is ours: without one spark of love on either side, and produced by circumstances which in general lead to coldness on one side and aversion on the other." (Byron - Letter to Thomas Moore)

Annabella's appearance and character were far removed from Byron's definition of his ideal woman and marriage partner. She was described as:

Dumpy, prudish and dowdy

Humourless with a pompous and pedantic style of expression

Superior and full of her own self-importance

Selfish and determined to have her way

An intellectual blue-stocking - *"The princess of parallelograms; his moral Clytemnestra."*

"She is a very superior woman, and very little spoiled, which is strange in an heiress; a girl of twenty; a peeress, that is to be, in her own right; an only child, and a savante, who has always had her own way. She is a poetess- a mathematician - a meta-physician; and yet, with all, very kind, generous." (Byron)

Her wounded pride and feelings of resentment would not permit a reconciliation. By 1815 Annabella refused to speak with Byron and she sought custody of their daughter Ada. Byron's response was captured in his poem *'Fare thee well'*:

"Fare the well! And if for ever,
Still for ever, fare thee well:
Even though unforgiving, never
'Gainst thee shall my heart rebel

When our child's first accents flow
Wilt thou teach her to say 'Father!
Though his care she must forego."

As soon as Byron left London Piccadilly, the bailiffs moved in and seized everything. Byron never saw Annabella again during the remaining eight years of his life. With the manuscripts amounting to Byron's autobiography burnt, the truth of his marriage and separation remains largely a matter of conjecture. In certain respects, Byron may have blamed himself for the separation. At the time of parting, he felt there had been *"no very deep sense of injury on either side."*

"Where there is blame it belongs to myself; and if I cannot redeem, I must bear it." (Byron - Letter to Thomas Moore)

"Not withstanding every thing I considered our re-union as not impossible - for more than a year after the separation - but then I gave up the hope entirely - and forever... (Byron - Letter to Lady Byron 1821)

Upon the death of Annabella's mother, in January 1822, it was Lord Byron who was required to take action. Although legally separated he was nevertheless obliged to incorporate the Noel coat of arms into his armorial bearings and he adopted the surname 'Noel Byron' in correspondence. All matters regarding the inheritance had been left undecided by the articles of separation and Byron felt himself entirely justified in adopting his approach:

"I have been made the victim of this woman's family - and have been absolutely ruined in reputation... I certainly did by no means marry her for her fortune, but if, after having undergone what I have, "Fortune (like Honour) comes unlooked for," - I feel by no means disposed to abandon my just claim to my just share; at the same time neither desiring nor requiring more than fair and honourable."(Byron - Letter to Douglas Kinnaird 1822)

Lady Byron committed her life to social causes such as prison reform and the abolition of the slave trade. She attended The World Anti Slavery Convention in 1840.

Claire Clairmont

Claire Clairmont, the stepsister of Mary Godwin, had a brief affair with Byron and became pregnant.

"I never loved or pretended to love – but a man is a man – and if a girl of 18 comes prancing to you at all hours – there is but one way"

Fig 54
Claire Mary Jane Clairmont by Amelia Curran 1819

Claire was a writer and acted as Byron's scribe, providing copies of his draft manuscripts for *Childe Harold.* She had accompanied Percy Bysshe Shelley and Mary Godwin to Switzerland and returned with them to England. Like them, Claire was an advocate of free love. She later claimed that her relationship with Byron had afforded her *"only a few minutes of pleasure, but a lifetime of trouble."*
In her seventies, she vindictively described Byron as:
"A human tyger slaking his thirst for inflicting pain upon defenceless women who had loved him." (a fragment of a memoir by Claire Clairmont discovered in 2010)

Initially called Alba, the baby girl was later christened Clara Allegra Byron. Claire and Alba settled in with the Shelleys. When this proved increasingly difficult, Byron agreed to take custody. He identified resemblances to himself, both in Allegra's appearance and her temperament.

"She is very pretty - remarkably intelligent - she has blue eyes - that singular forehead - fair curly hair - and a devil of a spirit. But that is Papa's." (Byron - Letter to Augusta Leigh 1818)

Teresa, Contessa Guiccioli

A woman of great charm and demure self-confidence, Teresa was well educated at a convent and loved literature. She was innately flirtatious and Byron's initial impression was of:

"a great coquette - with a good deal of imagination and some passion." (Byron)

Falling in love, Byron went on to value her for her fierce loyalty, originality and directness.

"The last and (with one single exception) only real love of his whole life." (Thomas Moore)

An intimate love which brought him peace and happiness. He had finally found the woman he had been searching for all his adult life.

Byron was accepted as her Cicisbeo - the escort or lover of a married woman with the knowledge and consent of the husband.

Fig 55
Teresa, Contessa Guiccioli
Drawing by A.E. Chalo

"I like women – but the more their system here (in Italy) develops upon me the worse it seems. The polygamy is all on the female side.

I have been an intriguer, a husband, a whoremonger, and now I am a cavalier servente – by the holy! It is a strange sensation." (Byron - Letter to Hobhouse 1819)

Lord Byron and Contessa Teresa Guiccoli

Fig 56
Lithograph by Regnier 1819

20c. Relationships with Men and Male Adolescents

Student Days
Whilst in England, there is no clear evidence of homosexual acts. Sodomy was illegal and punishable by death. It was thus a compelling reason to stay silent. Fagging in public schools was, however, prevalent in the 1800s.

It was Lady Caroline Lamb who claimed that Byron had told her about childhood relationships of a sexual nature with three other pupils at Harrow School. This was where his attraction to adolescent boys first became evident. He referred to his entourage of young pupils as his 'Theban band'. The most endearing and enduring friendship was with John FitzGibbon, 2nd Earl of Clare - four years his junior.

Byron spent some time at Newstead Abbey during the school holidays. In correspondence with his mother, Byron claimed that their tenant Lord Grey de Ruthyn, aged twenty three, had made some "aberrant sexual advances" which both offended and revolted the fifteen year old Byron.

William John Bankes was a lifelong friend of Lord Byron. They were together both at Harrow School and Cambridge University. He sometimes accompanied Byron on his Mediterranean Travels. His homosexual behaviour caused him to flee England in 1841.

It appeared in correspondence that whilst at Trinity College Cambridge, Byron was associated with a sophisticated group of like-minded friends, fascinated by the theory and practice of homosexuality. Members used a coded language - including abbreviations from Latin - to communicate amongst themselves.

Byron is known to have written romantic poems to John Edleston, John FitzGibbon (Lord Clare), and William Sackvile (Earl De La Warr).

John Edleston
Whilst at university, Byron met John Edleston (a fifteen-year-old chorister at Trinity), with whom he formed a homoerotic attachment - *"a violent though pure love and passion."* The poems he addressed to Edleston, using the deceptive female name of Thyrza, suggested a *"romantic aura of untouchable purity"* such that Edleston was - a *"youthful idol of unfulfilled desire."*

Byron was clearly upset when he left university and embarked upon his travels -
"Edleston and I have separated for the present and my mind is a chaos of hope and sorrow ... He has been my almost constant associate since 1805 when I entered Trinity College. His voice first

attracted my notice, his countenance fixed it and his manners attached him to me forever… I certainly love him more than any human being.'' (Byron)

Edleston thanked Byron for his patronage and 'parental kindness': *''I must beg leave to acknowledge the deep and grateful sense I have of the honour conferred on me by your Lordship's parental kindness; of which I shall cherish an everlasting remembrance… I must beg leave to repeat that it is only the favour of your Lordship's personal influence and patronage which I humbly presumed to request.''(John Edleston)*

It is unclear from Byron's writings whether or not the friendship was sexual. His letters were often sexually ambiguous.

Mediterranean Tour and self-exile

One of Byron's main motives in setting out on his travels appeared to be to avoid homophobic prejudice and participate in sexual contact with males in a more relaxed legal and moral context. Certain forms of bi-sexuality were accepted in those places where Byron spent time - notably Italy, Greece and Albania.

Despite the freedom various countries offered, there does not appear to be records of him being sexually involved with adult males during his self-imposed exile.

Nicolo Giraud

Once in Greece - and Athens in particular - Byron enjoyed greater sexual freedom under the more relaxed social and legal regimes. Byron stayed at the Capuchin monastery in Athens as a guest. Born c.1795 in Greece to French parents, Nicolo Giraud (aged c. fifteen) worked at the monastery.

He spoke Italian 'like a native' and Greek fluently and was assigned to help Byron practise both languages. Giraud became Byron's 'Dragoman' (interpreter) and 'Major-Domo' (chief steward) and they travelled together to the Peloponnese peninsula at the southern tip of the mainland. They finally parted company in Malta - an island in Southern Europe. Byron paid for his schooling in a monastery on the island and in his will, left Giraud £7,000 (about £500,000 in 2024) - which he later cancelled.

In the absence of clear evidence, the nature of the relationship between Lord Byron and Giraud remains a topic of speculation amongst biographers and scholars of Byron to this day. Some, including his early biographer Thomas Moore, believed the pair's interaction was platonic and another example of the homoerotic desire he had experienced with John Edleston.

"During this period of his stay in Greece we find him forming one of these extraordinary friendships - if attachment to persons so inferior to himself can be called by that name. It's happened before (the cottage boy near Newstead; the young chorister at Cambridge) – the pride of being a protector and the pleasure of exerting gratitude seems to have constituted to his mind the chief, pervading charm." (Thomas Moore)

Others (basing their perceptions on their own personal opinions and/or correspondence) argued that Byron engaged in sexual activity with Giraud. Byron described Nicolo as "the most beautiful being I have ever beheld."Details are scarce regarding their relationship. It appeared, however, that in letters to John Cam Hobhouse and other university friends, Byron stated that he had initially looked forward to, then enjoyed, and subsequently grown tired of 'pl and opt Cs'. - their code for unlimited sexual intercourse, taken from Petronius's Satyricon coitum plenum et optabilem.

Self-exile

Leaving England, Byron travelled through Switzerland and Italy with the Shelleys. The latter were advocates of communal living and free love. They wished to lead lives that were socially unacceptable in England. Both Shelley and Byron with their affinity for ancient Greece alluded to sexual acts between men in their poetry.

The Pisan Circle of Friends was formed in 1822. The Shelleys, George Byron, Thomas Medwin, Edward and Jane Williams and Edward John Trelawny all lived near each other and met regularly. The Circle embodied the meeting of 'kindred spirits' and 'soul mates'. However there is no evidence that sex was involved. The group may now be identified as (very) early precursors of the gay liberation movement.
"Drawn together by sexual affinities, that they discussed male love, and endeavoured to liberate it." (John Lauritsen, author)

Whilst in Venice, Byron took Giovanni Battista Falcieri (known as Tita) into his service. He was a handsome young gondolier - but again there is no evidence of sexual activity.

Byron clearly pursued a relationship with his page, **Loukas Chalandritsanos**, who gave no inkling of affection in return.

21. MAIN FINDINGS AND CONCLUSIONS

Background

I set out with the intention of walking in Byron's footsteps - both at home and abroad, with the aim of establishing the true facts and unravelling the myths which continue to surround his life. I have to admit that this was a somewhat unrealistic goal as his final memoirs were destroyed and those who knew him well had little to say regarding certain key issues. Byron was however, a prolific correspondent and we do have the memoirs, journals and correspondence of his contemporaries - be they friend or foe.

Appearance and imagery

We have a pretty good insight into Byron's physical appearance, his strengths and weaknesses and how he manipulated his image. Whilst his 'club foot' may have stopped him from executing the rhythmic movements of the waltz, it certainly did not stop him from excelling at swimming, boxing, fencing and pistol shooting. As a result of the discrepancy in his lower limbs and the asymmetry of his eyes, Byron's portraits very rarely show his full body length and his head is almost always turned to the right. He was preoccupied with his weight and body shape, so much so that his approach to food may be considered to constitute bulimia.

Character and personality

Byron was clearly a perfectionist. His deep thinking introspective approach to problem-solving suggests that he was also a 'Ruminator', and that this could lead to over-thinking, stress, anxiety and depression. The mood swings with episodes of extreme highs and lows suggests that he would now be classified as bi-polar. He was also somewhat introverted and struggled with social-phobia.

In 2024, in the modern healthcare context, he would also have been considered a potential 'Misophoniac' who exhibited a reflexive response of agitation, anger, or rage, to certain specific noises made by others.

Sexuality

Byron's sexual orientation has long been a difficult and contentious topic to broach. Those who seek to discuss it must to some degree speculate as, without his memoires, evidence is often vague or contentious. The modern definition of our 'Casanova of The Romantics' would be pansexual or omnisexual. In the early 1800s his behaviour would have been described as that of a bi-sexual. Before judging Lord Byron, it is important to understand the different laws and moralities pertaining to the countries in which he lived during his lifetime.

I can only summarise my own personal opinions on Byron's relationships and sexuality. On this occasion, viewed in chronological order:
- Byron, aged only eleven, wrote to John Hanson (his guardian and solicitor) complaining that May Gray (his nurse) was sexually and physically abusive toward him.
- Fagging in public schools was prevalent and George Byron was a popular fag-master and friend.
- It was not unusual for university students to want to explore their sexuality further. Women's colleges were not founded until the 1860s.
- The relationship with John Edleston may have been sexual or homoerotic.
- Byron's adolescent love for Mary Chaworth was rejected. Had she gone on to marry him, both their lives could have been very different.

- Augusta Leigh was Byron's half-sister. Incest was not illegal in England until 1908. One can only speculate whether Byron fathered Medora Leigh.
- Most of the areas of Italy had eliminated all criminal and civil laws concerning sodomy.
- The role of Cavalier Servente was commonplace (in the higher echelons of Italian society).
- Byron's contemporaries argued over whether his relationship with Nicolo Giraud in Greece was sexual or homoerotic. If one considers it to be most likely sexual, then its legality would be dependent on whether Nicolo, at the age of fourteen or fifteen, had undergone puberty.
- After the publication of *Childe Harold's Pilgrimage* Byron was besieged by women. The most famous was his very public affair with Lady Caroline Lamb. She effectively ruined his reputation by claiming that he was 'Mad, Bad and Dangerous to know' and writing her defamatory book Glenarvon.
- His marriage to Anne Isabella Milbanke lasted only a year. She 'failed to reform him' and demanded a legal separation and custody of their child.
- Claire Clairmont, the stepsister of Mary Shelley, had a brief affair with Byron and became pregnant. Their daughter Allegra died in a convent in Italy, at the age of five.
- Contessa Teresa Guiccioli proved (at least initially) to be the woman Byron had been searching for all his adult life. He was her Cavalier Servente.

Byronic Poet
The Byronic hero was the poet's own far-reaching brand of Romanticism. Its lasting appeal is largely down to the depth and complexity of the hero's character. Some will say that the ultimate Byronic superhero is Batman - highly intelligent but volatile, violent and self-destructive with a tendency to rebel against authority.

Younger readers may well be thinking more in terms of Severus Snape in J.K.Rowling's Harry Potter.

Warring Lord

Byron has been aptly described as a Liberal Whig, a Political Rebel and Intellectual Revolutionary. Warring with words, he made his maiden speech in the House of Lords, opposing the harsh Tory measures against the Luddites. He frequently spoke out against 'wars of aggression for personal gain' and for 'liberty' and 'equality'. His actions during the Greek War of Independence reflected his total and undying commitment to The Cause:

"I have given her my time, my means, my health, — and now I give her my life! — what could I do more?"

Byron was a hard core Philhellene influenced by the Age of Enlightenment and his Grand Tour of the Mediterranean. In Greece he reinvented himself as a Political Statesman of the New Age.

Byron's Death in Missolonghi

Lord Byron died on the 19th April 1824 at the age of thirty-six. It is more than likely that he died of Plasmodium Falciparum (the only one of the four types of malaria to affect the brain) and exsanguination (significant blood loss) resulting from repeated bleeding.

Byron's War Legacy

The death of Lord Byron secured both increased involvement from western nations, and the union of Greek factions, against the Ottoman Empire. The Turkish Egyptian fleet was annihilated at the naval battle of Navarino. In 1830 the founding of an independent Greek State was recognised by the Great Powers and the eight year war against Ottoman rule came to an end.

Fig 57
The Advocate and Supporter of the Greek Nation
by Adam Friedel c1830

Byron is recognised as 'a hero' 'a saviour' and 'a deliverer' by the Greek people who had wanted Byron to be buried in Missolonghi or the Temple of Theseus on the hill of the Acropolis. On the 19th April 2008, Greece announced Byron's Day as a public holiday. Greek children are taught from a young age how Byron died fighting for their country's freedom. Statues of the poet adorn multiple cities. *"Nobody would think of a free Greece without thinking at the same time of Lord Byron." (Greek Prime Minister, Eleftherios Venizelos 1931)*

Dual Personality

Byron had two very different dissociative identities.

The first identity is of a renowned 'Genius of Poetry' and 'Casanova of the Romantics' - arguably, literature's most illustrious sex symbol. A man of ambiguous and fluid sexuality and pioneer of sexual liberation, the bi-sexual aspect of his character was exposed through his unrequited search for true love.

The second identity was strongly influenced by the Grand Tour and the Age of Enlightenment. These invoked the emergence of a rebellious fighter who actively supported nationalism in Europe - namely Italy and Greece. A heroic statesman of a new age, a Philhellene and ultimately, on the 19th April 1824, a 'martyr to the cause of Greek Liberty'.

Recognition in his Homeland
Byron's body was returned to England on the brig Florida. His friends had envisaged a triumphant burial in Westminster Abbey or St Paul's Cathedral. Due to his reputation, his coffin and statue were refused. His wish to be buried at Newstead Abbey in the tomb alongside his dog Boatswain was ignored and his body was interred in the family vault at the Church in Hucknall Torkard, Nottinghamshire.

The statue designed for Poet's Corner in Westminster Abbey was eventually placed in the Wren Library at Trinity College, Cambridge.

In England 2024, the words of Giuseppe Mazzini still resound:
"England, will one day feel how ill it is - not for Byron, but for herself - that the foreigner who lands upon her shores should search in vain for that temple which should be her national Parthenon for the poet beloved and admired by the nations of Europe." (Giuseppe Mazzini; Italian Politician 1805-1872)

Children will not discover Lord Byron on their school curriculum. They will however find Percy Bysshe Shelley and *'Ozymandias'*. This point was made by Ken Purslow twenty-five years ago at an international Byron Society Conference:
"In Britain he is not even taught in schools, unlike the United States and Japan. They are only now thinking of putting him on the national curriculum in Britain. It's a disgrace." (Ken Purslow, Head of the International Byron Society at Newstead Abbey)

With the bicentennial anniversary of his death now upon us, surely that time has arrived. In the meantime, the online Kids Encyclopedia 'Kpedia Kiddle' is powered by Google Safe Search. 'Lord Byron Facts for Kids' https://kids.kiddle.co/Lord_Byron provides a thorough and easy-going investigation of Byron's life and legacy.

In London, the statue of Byron by Richard Belt sits on the red and white marble pedestal presented by the Greek government, and stands at the south end of London's Park Lane on a traffic island. Now separated from Hyde Park, it is in poor condition and no longer readily accessible to the public.

The Byron Society aims to raise sufficient funds to restore and move the Byron Memorial Statue.

Byron statue once restored and relocated in Hyde Park

For more information, scan the JustGiving QR Code on the back cover or visit www.justgiving.com/campaign/sos-byron-memorial

The roof of Newstead Abbey, Byron's ancestral home, is in dire need of repair. The Newstead Abbey Partnership raises funds to preserve Newstead Abbey's past and secure its future. For more information visit: www.justgiving.com/newsteadabbeypartnership

ADDENDUM: NEWSTEAD ABBEY

1. The Wildman Legacy

Colonel Thomas Wildman (1787-1859) approved the purchase of Newstead Abbey in December 1817, whilst Lord Byron was living in Venice. It was ratified in 1818. The estate sold for £94,500. The bicentennial price would be approaching £7 million. Thomas Wildman, a retired officer of the 7th Hussars, virtually re-built and refurbished Newstead Abbey at an estimated cost of some £100,000 (£10+ million).

An outstanding legacy and tribute to Lord Byron - he is recognised as 'the man who saved Byron's home' and re-created Newstead Abbey as a shrine to his memory. His restoration work remains with us to this day.

"Wildman saved the house from destruction and turned it into one of the most magnificent and interesting seats in England."

Thomas Wildman in his favourite Army uniform - The 7th Queen's Own Hussars; Cavalry regiment in the British Army.

Fig 58
Thomas Wildman (1787-1859)
by James Lonsdale

The origins of wealth

The Wildman family originally lived in Lancashire. In the early 18th Century, Lancaster was a port engaged in the West India trade in sugar, rum and slaves. James Beckford Wildman (1789-1867) developed the Quebec Sugar Estate in St. Mary Parish and went on to own three other estates in Jamaica. The Quebec Estate was one of the largest sugar plantations in Jamaica with over 800 slaves. Upon his return to England, he purchased Chilham Castle near Canterbury.

Thomas Wildman was the eldest son of Thomas and Sarah Wildman of Bacton Hall in Suffolk, Bedford Square in London (and others). At the age of nine, he inherited his father's estates in Jamaica and Britain. He was educated at Harrow School where he first met George Byron. His alma mater was Christ Church College, Oxford from where he matriculated in 1806.

Military career

Coming into his inheritance in 1808 at the age of twenty-one, Thomas Wildman joined the Army. He received a cornet in the 7th Hussars and was promoted to Lieutenant. He fought in the Peninsular and Napoleonic Wars. He was aide-de-camp to the Earl of Uxbridge and wounded when the latter lost his leg at the battle of Waterloo. He subsequently joined the 9th Light Dragoons where he was promoted to Colonel. He was equerry to the Duke of Sussex and retired from the Army in 1832.

In 1816, he married Louisa Preisig (1801-1877), daughter of F. Preizig of Appenzal in Switzerland. They had no children.

Rebuild of Newstead Abbey

Thomas Wildman and Louisa, along with her sister Caroline, moved into Newstead Abbey. Wildman employed architect John Shaw to reform the house and introduce Colsa oil lighting and water closets. The aim was to re-invent the house in a more accurate (Tudor) Gothic style. Central to the rebuild were:
- the removal of the external staircase and hall entrance. Thus the main entrance was moved to the ground floor, necessitating two new staircases at either end of the building and an extra square bay window
- the Great Hall, now with a new roof and chimney piece was once again habitable. Heraldic glass windows, commemorating his mother and the military careers of himself and his brothers, were added
- a new 'Glastonbury' style kitchen with an octagonal pyramid roof replaced the old priory kitchen
- a re-modelling of the South Front, South East and East Wings
- the addition of the Sussex Tower
- relocation of the gothic fountain back into the cloister garth
- a family gallery in the chapel

Life at Newstead Abbey

Thomas Wildman was appointed Lord Lieutenant of Nottinghamshire and took command of the Sherwood Rangers. He was Captain of the Mansfield troop of Nottinghamshire Yeomanry. He served as High Sheriff of Nottinghamshire 1821-22.

Equerry to the Duke of Sussex, he was the provincial Grand Master of the Freemasons. The Duke of Sussex was Grand Master of the United Lodge of England and tended to spend six weeks each year at Newstead Abbey.

Thomas Wildman was a part of the politically like-minded upper classes who held strong radical opinions. He was seen as a Liberal Tory and described as -
'One of a benevolent landowning class who fought for the people from elaborately feudal castles or gothic mansions.'

Byron referred to him as a "Man of honour."

Wildman died in 1859 at the age of seventy-two. Upon his death, Lady Preisig Wildman (1801-1877) moved to Lenton Hall. Newstead Abbey was sold to William Frederick Webb.

2. The Webb Family

William Frederick Webb (1829-1899) inherited properties in Yorkshire and Lincolnshire from his uncles as well as the Westwick Estate in County Durham from his father Frederick Webb. One of four children, he was raised in France and educated at Eton. He joined the army and became a captain of the 17th Lancers. He soon resigned as he did not enjoy regimental life.

At the age of twenty-two, along with William Wyndham Codrington, he travelled to South Africa to hunt big game and explore the country. The natives called him M'Tuffa (Giraffe) as he was some 6ft 4inches tall. During his time in South Africa, he became very ill (most likely malaria). Without medical aid, he would have died had not Dr. Livingstone (the Scottish missionary doctor, explorer and abolitionist) treated him, cured him and effectively saved his life.

Fig59
AfterThe Lion Hunt
an imagined scene
by Alfred Corbould 1857

''My acquaintance with Mr Webb began in Africa, where he was a daring and successful hunter, and his continued friendship is most valuable, because he has seen missionary work.'' (Dr Livingstone Preface to Expedition to the Zambesi 1865)

Webb returned to England and married Emilia Jane Goodlake in 1857. The couple moved to Yorkshire where their first three children were born - Augusta Zelia (1858), Geraldine Catherine (1860) and Wilfred (born and died in 1861). The family moved into Newstead Abbey, where four more children were born - Ethel Mary (1862), Mabel Cecelia (1863), Algernon Frederick (1865) and Roderick Beauclerk (1867). Algernon committed suicide at the age of nineteen and Roderick was exiled to Australia - an undischarged bankrupt.

William Frederick Webb built gasworks on the Newstead estate and introduced 19th century gas lighting, radiators and a hot water heating system. He built:
- the new Stable Block in a Victorian Gothic style. It included an infirmary, smithy and living quarters for stable staff
- a new Main Lodge on Mansfield Road and other lodges including a Gardener's Cottage
- the Chapel was completely transformed and windows replaced with stained glass
 - the plaster was stripped from the cloister walks

Dr Livingstone stayed in the Sussex Tower at Newstead Abbey whilst in England writing about his famous explorations and in particular, 'the Narrative of an Expedition to the Zambesi and its tributaries'. The Orangery was used as both a billiard room and storage facility for Livingstone's fossils and geological specimens.
"Mr. and Mrs. Webb, my much-loved friends, wrote to Bombay inviting me, in the event of my coming to England, to make Newstead Abbey my headquarters, and upon my arrival renewed their invitation: and though, when I accepted it, I had no intention of remaining so long with my kind-hearted generous friends, I stayed with them until April 1865,and under their roof transcribed from my

own and my brother's journal the whole of this present book. It is with heartfelt gratitude I would record their unwearied kindness." (Dr Livingstone: Preface to Mission to the Zambesi 1865)

Following the death of their mother in South Africa, Geraldine and Ethel travelled extensively, returning to Newstead with paper screens and souvenirs from Japan. They created a private sitting room and filled it with souvenirs from Japan and China. Their passion extended into the gardens. Ethel was inspired by landscape gardening in Japan and incorporated waterfalls, a tea house and a Torii gate into the design. Trees, plants and garden sculptures were imported directly from a Japanese garden centre.

In later life, William Frederick Webb developed an interest in Egyptology. He died of laryngitis in Luxor in 1899. Upon his death, Newstead Abbey passed to Geraldine. She married Sir Herbert Charles Chermside and returned with him to South Africa where he was based. Ethel Webb remained in charge of Newstead whilst her sister and husband were abroad. She was responsible for further restoration work.
- the vaulted priory warming room was split into two and named the Plantagenet and Becket rooms

- two additional stories were added to the service wing
- work on the Orangery included an extended rectangular bay window
- Byron's dressing room was stripped down to the bare stonework. Plans for a gothic style panelled room were abandoned when war broke out in 1914 and Ethel Webb died the following year

Geraldine's will had stipulated that whilst the Abbey should go to her sister Augusta, the contents would go to her husband.

Augusta was married to Philip Affleck Fraser, a civil engineer. She had a keen interest in Lord Byron and bought back those items she felt should never have left Newstead Abbey in the first place. This included the Phillips portrait and his bed. She furnished the South East Wing and established it as a self-contained unit.

When their son, Charles Ian Fraser came of age, she transferred the property to him. In 1930 he decided to sell the Newstead Estate. The Hucknall Colliery Co. purchased the coal royalties and Sir Julian Cahn - the Nottingham entrepreneur and philanthropist - purchased much of the property. One condition of the sale was that Cahn would present the property to the nation. However the National Trust expressed no interest, and Nottingham City Council stepped in - even though Newstead Abbey was located some ten miles outside the city boundary!

ACKNOWLEDGEMENTS

I must give special thanks to my fellow volunteers at Newstead Abbey, Trish Davis and Amanda Gibbons, for their continuous support throughout the process and for sharing their in-depth knowledge of Lord Byron acquired during their years working at Newstead Abbey and through their connections with the Newstead Abbey Byron Society.

To Emily Paterson-Morgan at the London Byron Society for her advice, help and support.

To Geoffrey Bond, author of Mad Bad and Dangerous to Show and other contemporary books on Lord Byron, for his inspiration, encouragement and advice.

To Andrew Stauffer, author of Byron A Life in Ten Letters for his mentorship of a fellow bicentennial biographer.

To IDA Johnston for his interaction on medical conundrums.

To Mick Smurthwaite, Site Manager of Newstead Abbey and Simon Brown, Curator, for their assistance and permission to photograph inside Newstead Abbey.

To Dr Sam Hirst, Research Fellow on Byron, for her help on Byron's poetical works.

To Dan and Byron for taking photographs in and around Newstead Abbey and providing many of the illustrations.

To Rosa Florou, President of the Messolonghi Byron Society for her time and kindness during my visit. For showing me around Messolonghi and arranging for me to meet the curators at The National Historical Museum in Athens, where I was able to obtain an excellent insight into the Greek War of Independence.

And the production team:
To Martin Bryant, for his initial advice on format, content and publishing.
To Martin Gibbons, software engineer for his time and production skills.
To Jo Boyer for designing the front cover.
To Morgan Richardson for his design of the back cover.
To my husband and all those friends, colleagues and acquaintances who have subsequently reviewed and proof-read the content.

SOURCE MATERIAL

The knowledge I have gained in order to compile this booklet has come from many sources.

Books I have bought and read or dipped into. Chiefly:

The Works of Lord Byron Vol 1 and 11 by William Anderson Esq.
Byron: A Life in Ten Letters by Andrew Stauffer
Byron's War by Roderick Beaton
Byron at Burgage Manor 1803-08 by Geoffrey Bond
Dangerous To Show: Byron and His Portraits by Geoffrey Bond & Christine Kenyon Jones
Newstead Abbey 1540-1931 by Rosalys Coope and Peter Smith
Fall of the House of Byron by Emily Brand
Shades of Heroes by David Newport
Lord Byron Series by Gretta Curran Browne on Kindle Unlimited
The Greek Adventure by David Howarth
Byron: Life and Legend by Fiona MacCarthy
In the Winds Eye - Byron's Letters and Journals Edited by Leslie A. Marchand
In My Hot Youth - Byron's Letters and Journals Edited by Leslie A. Marchand
The sayings of Lord Byron by Stoddard Martin
The Last Days of Lord Byron by William Parry
Lord Byron's Last Journey to Greece - Journal of Count Pietro Gamba
Finden's illustrations of the Life and Works of Lord Byron
The Greek Poets Praise 'The Britannic Muse' by M. Byron Raizis online

The internet has been crucial to an in-depth investigation of the life and times of Lord Byron.

ILLUSTRATIONS

Fig 1 Statue of George Gordon, Lord Byron by Bertel Thorvaldsen 1830-34. Alamy stock photo

Fig 2 Admiral 'Foul-Weather Jack' Byron by Joshua Reynolds c.1748. Courtesy of Newstead Abbey, Nottingham City Museums and Galleries

Fig 3 Mrs Catherine Gordon Byron by Thomas Stewardson. Courtesy of Newstead Abbey, Nottingham City Museums and Galleries

Fig 4 Augusta Mary Leigh by James Holmes. Alamy stock photo

Fig 5 Ada King, Countess of Lovelace by Margaret Carpenter. Courtesy of Newstead Abbey, Nottingham City Museums and Galleries

Fig 6 Lord George Gordon Byron as a child. Steel engraving by H.Payne, after Leipzig Vidal. Alamy stock photo

Fig 7 Watercolour portrait miniature of Lord Byron by Girolamo Prepiani. Courtesy of Newstead Abbey, Nottingham City Museums and Galleries

Fig 8 Byron in Undergraduate dress; Anonymous c.1806. Alamy stock photo

Fig 9 George Gordon 6th. Baron Byron oil on canvas by Thomas Griffiths Wainewright. Courtesy of Newstead Abbey, Nottingham City Museums and Galleries

Fig 10 George Noel Gordon Byron by Charles Turner from the painting by William West (Pisa 1822). Courtesy of Newstead Abbey, Nottingham City Museums and Galleries

Fig 11 Print of silhouette of George Gordon Noel Byron cut by Marrianne Kent, Mrs Leigh Hunt in 1822. Courtesy of Newstead Abbey, Nottingham City Museums and Galleries

Fig 12 George Gordon, 6th Lord Byron by Thomas Phillips 1813. Courtesy of Newstead Abbey, Nottingham City Museums and Galleries

Fig 13 Lord Byron in Albanian dress by Thomas Phillips 1813. Courtesy of Newstead Abbey, Nottingham City Museums and Galleries

Fig 14 Hand coloured lithograph of Lord Byron by R.Martin; Published by Adam Friedel in 1827. Courtesy of Newstead Abbey, Nottingham City Museums and Galleries

Fig 15 Miniature after Sanders.
Courtesy of Newstead Abbey, Nottingham City Museums and Galleries
Fig 16 Miniature by Girolamo Prepiani in scarlet military costume.
Courtesy of Newstead Abbey, Nottingham City Museums and Galleries
Fig 17 Bust of Lord Byron by Edward Hodges Baily R.A. c.1826.
Courtesy of Newstead Abbey, Nottingham City Museums and Galleries
Fig 18 George Gordon Byron carved bust by Bertel Thorvaldsen 1817.
Thorvaldsens Museum, Copenhagen. Alamy stock photo
Fig 19 Lord Byron at the age of seven. Engraving by Edward Finden after
watercolour by William Kay of Edinburgh 1795. Alamy stock photo
Fig 20 George Gordon Noel Byron amongst the ruins at Newstead.
Alamy stock photo
Fig 21 Lord Byron when at Cambridge. Watercolour drawing by Gilchrist.
Courtesy of Newstead Abbey, Nottingham City Museums and Galleries
Fig 22 West View at Newstead Abbey.
Courtesy of Newstead Abbey, Nottingham City Museums and Galleries
Fig 23 Lord Byron and his favourite. Popular Portrait Gallery.
Courtesy of Newstead Abbey, Nottingham City Museums and Galleries
Fig 24 Portrait of Boatswain by Clifton Tomson.
Courtesy of Newstead Abbey, Nottingham City Museums and Galleries
Fig 25 Boatswain's Memorial tomb at Newstead Abbey.
Fig 26 Lord Byron oil on canvas by Richard Westall 1813.
Courtesy of Newstead Abbey, Nottingham City Museums and Galleries
Fig 27 George Gordon Byron, 6th Baron Byron. Engraving by Henry Meyer
after George Henry Harlow c.1815.
Courtesy of Newstead Abbey, Nottingham City Museums and Galleries
Fig 28 The Newstead Abbey Byron Society 1988-2023.
Fig 29 George Gordon, 6th Lord Byron oil on canvas by George Sanders.
Commissioned by Lord Byron in 1807. Alamy stock photo
Fig 30 Interior view of the Lysicrates Monument incorporated within the
Capuchin Monastery. Engraving by Charles Heath from a drawing by S.
Pomardi.
Courtesy of Newstead Abbey, Nottingham City Museums and Galleries

Fig 31 West view at Newstead Abbey by Peter Tillemans
Courtesy of Newstead Abbey, Nottingham City Museums and Galleries
Fig 32 Childe Harold's Pilgrimage. Coloured engraving from an 1850 edition. Alamy stock photo
Fig 33 The Giaour by Eugene Delacroix 1826. Alamy stock photo
Fig 34 Don Juan et Haidee dans La Grotto.
Courtesy of Newstead Abbey, Nottingham City Museums and Galleries
Fig 35 Byron's Oak. Nottingham City Council photograph
Fig 36 Lord Byron sat dreaming by the Peachy Tomb in St. Mary's Graveyard, Harrow-on-the-Hill. Alamy stock photo
Fig 37 Imaginary recreation of the cremation of Percy Bysshe Shelley by Louis Fournier. Alamy stock photo
Fig 38 Kolokotronis by Dionysiops Tsokos. In the public domain
Fig 39 Prince Alexandros Mavrokordatos by Adam Friedel. In the public domain
Fig 40 Princess Manto Mavrogenous by Adam Friedel. In the public domain.
Fig 41 The reception of Lord Byron at Missolonghi. Oil on canvas by Theodoros Vryzakis 1861. Alamy stock photo
Fig 42 Illustration by Robert Seymour from The Last days of Lord Byron by William Parry.
Fig 43 Illustration by Robert Seymour from The Last days of Lord Byron by William Parry.
Fig 44 View from Lord Byron's House in Missolonghi by H.Raper. Alamy stock photo
Fig 45 Interior of St. Mary Magdalene Church.
Courtesy of Newstead Abbey, Nottingham City Museums and Galleries
Fig 46 John Cam Hobhouse, 1st Baron Broughton. Engraving by J. Hopwood 1834. Published by J Murray. Alamy stock photo
Fig 47 Letter to Hobhouse.
Fig 48 Joseph Murray by Thomas Barber.
Courtesy of Newstead Abbey, Nottingham City Museums and Galleries
Fig 49 Percy Bysshe Shelley. Engraving by William Finden from original portrait by Amelia Curran. Alamy stock photo

Fig 50 Mary Shelley by Richard Rothwell 1840. Alamy stock photo

Fig 51 Mary Ann Chaworth Musters by Thomas Phillips

Courtesy of Newstead Abbey, Nottingham City Museums and Galleries

Fig 52 Lady Caroline Lamb. Engraving by Henry Meyer.

Courtesy of Newstead Abbey, Nottingham City Museums and Galleries

Fig 53 Anne Isabella Noel Byron. Engraving by William Finden.

Alamy stock photo

Fig 54 Claire Mary Jane Clairmont by Amelia Curran 1819.

Courtesy of Newstead Abbey, Nottingham City Museums and Galleries

Fig 55 Teresa, Contessa Guiccioli. Drawing by AE Chalon.

Courtesy of Newstead Abbey, Nottingham City Museums and Galleries

Fig 56 Lord Byron and Contessa Teresa Guiccoli. Lithograph by Regnier.

Alamy stock photo

Fig 57 Lord Byron. The advocate and supporter of the Greek nation by Adam Friedel. In the public domain

Fig 58 Thomas Wildman (1787-1859) by James Lonsdale

Courtesy of Newstead Abbey, Nottingham City Museums and Galleries

Fig 59 After The Lion Hunt (W.F. Webb and Captain W. Codrington, South Africa). An imagined scene by Alfred Corbould 1857

Courtesy of Newstead Abbey, Nottingham City Museums and Galleries

Printed in Great Britain
by Amazon